Dragon Tales

A Collection of Chinese Stories

Panda Books

Panda Books
First Edition 1988
Second Printing 1990
Third Printing 1994

ISBN 7-5071-0024-3
ISBN 0-8351-2058-9

Published by CHINESE LITERATURE PRESS
Beijing 100037, China
Distributed by China International Book Trading Corporation
35 Chegongzhuang Xilu, Beijing 100044, China
P.O. Box 399, Beijing, China
Printed in the People's Republic of China

CONTENTS

Preface

FOR all that it has never been seen, references to that mystic creature of ancient legend the dragon abound in the Chinese classics, and besides the *Book of Changes*' "dragon flying in the sky", folk legends such as that of the flood dragon's journey to the sea have prompted speculation that the dragon was in antiquity a tribal totem whose image has over the centuries been enriched and taken on new guises to the point where it has a diversity of forms, each with its appropriate designation.

Described in legend as unique, miraculous and protean, the dragon has the ability to raise floods, bring thunder and lightning, summon up storms and transform itself at will; its mighty power is seen as the embodiment of all that is imposing and majestic. And the sovereigns of old China, no doubt in a bid to enlist the creature's limitless awe, likened themselves to embodiments of the dragon, clothing themselves in its almighty dignity. Thus the dragon became the symbol of princely power, acquiring by a deal of spurious analogy a concomitant sanctity proof against all blasphemy.

Yet to the minds of the common people it suggested, far from dread, an omen of good luck and fortune, an object of love and praise and the matter of many an excellent tale and legend down the ages.

The thirty-five stories collected here, drawn partly from classical literature and partly from traditional popular legend, include the tale of the ascent to heaven on a dragon's back of Huang Di, the race ancestor of the Chinese, a legend hoary enough to have been quoted in the first century BC in Sima Qian's *Records of the Historian* and one which was to exert a far-reaching influence on the dragon's position in after ages. Yet the genre which endeared itself most and spread farthest was that of the dragoness, and this has been much pored over by folklorists and students of popular literature. Current among many of the peoples of China in variations according to their several manners and customs, this has provoked immortal pieces from the brushes of the past, prominent among them Li Chaowei's "The Dragon King's Daughter" in the Tang Dynasty. Pu Songling's "The Rakshas and the Sea Market" is a powerful Qing Dynasty reworking of this theme, where the writer attacks the iniquities of the feudal system via the medium of a weird narrative of the dragon palace beneath the waves, where the dragon woman is a picture of oriental charm, virtuous in her beauty, urbane in her passion and punctilious towards love. "Li Jing" here ingeniously tells how man took over the function of the legendary dragon as a bringer of rain; "Short-Tailed Old Li" with its fight between the black dragon and the white dragon is a prime example of the many myths linking the names of mountains and rivers with dragons: these and many others, like the legend still current among the Dai that the dragon is the guardian of the village, are thought-provoking stories with a strong and curious appeal.

This volume may help to probe the mystery of how

and why the dragon, through all the natural accretions of cultural history millennia long, came to symbolize the spirit of the Chinese people.

Li Jing

IN the Tang Dynasty there was a Duke of Weiguo called Li Jing. Before becoming an official he used to go out hunting on Mount Lingshan, staying and having his meals there. The villagers wondered at him and would offer him rich food. With the passage of time they became close friends.

One day, coming across a herd of deer, he gave chase. The sun set, but he did not give up. As it was getting dark, he lost his way and could not get back. Foiled in his attempt, he was very vexed as he walked, but looking into the distance he discovered lamplight. He quickly made his way towards it. Reaching the place, he saw it was a mansion with a vermilion gate and surrounded by high walls. He knocked at the gate for a while until a man came out and asked who he was. Li Jing replied that he had lost his way and asked if he might put up in the mansion for the night.

"Our young masters are out," the man said. "Only the old lady is in. You may not come in."

Li Jing asked him to plead with the mistress. The man went in and reported, then returned. "She did not consent to your request at first, but considering that it is dark and you have lost your way, she has perforce to receive you."

So he was invited in. In a while a maid came. "Her

Ladyship," she announced.

About fifty, she wore a black skirt and white jacket and was possessed of an aristocratic grace.

Li Jing advanced and bowed to her.

"My sons are out," she said, returning his courtesy. "I should not have let you in, but it is too dark and you have lost your way. If I refused your request, where would you go? We dwell in the mountains. When my sons come home tonight there will be a commotion. I hope you will not be alarmed."

Soon the table was laid. The dishes set on it were fresh and delicious, with fish predominating. After the meal, the old lady retired. Two maids came bringing him clean, scented bedding and quilts, closed the door and fastened it, then left. Li Jing pondered over what had happened in the mountains. Night had fallen when he heard a noise outside. Wondering, he did not dare go to bed but sat up to listen. At midnight he heard hurried knocks at the gate and a response:

"The Heavenly decree has arrived. Your elder son is to send down rain for seven hundred li around the mountains, all by the fifth watch, none to stand or do any damage."

The respondent took the decree in and presented it to the lady.

Then the old lady was heard saying, "Neither of my sons has come back yet, and the decree to send the rain has arrived. We can not refuse it, and to postpone it would be to risk punishment. It is even too late to get word to him now. The servants aren't entitled to do it. What shall I do?"

"I found the visitor just now out of the common run," suggested a maid. "Shall we ask him to do it?"

Pleased, the lady went to knock at the door in person. "Have you gone to bed, young man? Come out for a moment, please."

Li Jing consented and went down the steps to meet her.

"This is not a residence of mortals, but a dragon palace," said the old lady. "My elder son is away at a wedding in the East Sea and my younger is escorting his sister, just when a Heavenly decree has arrived for rain to be sent down. They are more than ten thousand li away and could not be here in time even on cloud-back. Nor can I appoint others. May I ask you to take his place for the time being? Will you do that?"

"As a mortal, I cannot ride clouds. How shall I send down the rain? Teach me and I will," said Li Jing.

"If you do just as I say, you cannot go wrong," she said, and directed a page-boy to saddle a piebald horse and fetch a vessel, a little pot for the rain, which she had tied to the saddle. "As you ride," she warned him, "give the horse its head, and when it gallops and neighs, draw a drop of water from the pot and drop it on the mane. Be sure not to drop more than that."

Mounting, Li Jing hastened away. Suddenly he felt the horse rise and was surprised at its speed, as he was not aware that he was in the air. The wind was whirring past like an arrow, and thunder rumbled under his feet. Wherever it swelled, he dropped water. Suddenly through a rift in the clouds torn open by the lightning he caught sight of the village which he had stayed in.

"I put those villagers too much trouble," he thought. "Though they were very kind to me, I never repaid them. They are suffering from a burning drought, and the standing crops will be scorched. Now the rain is in my hand, I must at least give them some water."

Calculating that one drop would not be enough to moisten the fields, he sent down twenty in succession. After a little the rain was finished, and he rode back, to find the lady weeping in the reception room.

"What a mess you have made!" she complained. "I told you to send down only one drop. What did you mean by pouring it twenty feet deep? A drop amounts to a foot of rain on the ground. By midnight the village was twenty feet deep. Not a soul will be seen there again. I have been reproved and received eighty lashes. See how my back is covered with bloodstains. And my sons are involved too. Are you convinced now?"

Chagrined and terror-stricken, Li Jing could not even give an answer.

"You are an earthling," continued the old lady. "You cannot understand the changes of cloud and rain, so I bear you no grudge. But I am afraid lest the Master Dragon should come here for you. He is a terror! Flee, quickly! But you have done me a favour, and I have not repaid you. Here in the mountains I have nothing but two slaves to offer you. You can take both of them or choose only one."

Presently two maidservants were ordered out. One came from the east corridor, elegant and pleasing to the eye, the other from the west, wearing an angry frown and standing there sullenly.

"I'm a hunter," thought Li Jing, "given to fighting with wild animals. If I choose a maidservant to please me, others will consider me a coward." So he said to the lady, "I will not take both. Since you offer me either, I prefer the scowling one."

"As you wish," said the lady with a smile.

Then he bowed to her and departed, with the maid-servant following behind. After a few paces, he turned and found that the mansion had vanished from sight, and so had the maid. He had no choice but to find his way back alone. When it was daylight, he saw that the village had become a wilderness of waters with only the tips of the branches of the biggest trees showing and not a soul to be seen.

Later he rose to military power, vanquishing invaders and accomplishing great things, but he never attained the rank of premier, no doubt because he had mistakenly chosen only one of the two slaves. The saying that premiers come from east of the pass and generals from the west does not in fact allude to directions. What was said of the slaves predicted his future: if he had taken both, he would have risen from general to premier.

Translated by Song Shouquan

The Dragon King's Daughter

DURING the Yi Feng period (AD 676-678), a scholar named Liu Yi failed in the official examination and, as he was returning to the Xiang River Valley, decided to go and take his leave of a fellow provincial who was staying at Jingyang. He had ridden about two miles when a bird flying up from the ground startled his horse and made it bolt, and it galloped two miles before he could stop it. Then he caught sight of a girl herding sheep by the roadside. She was amazingly beautiful but her finely arched eyebrows were knit, her clothes were soiled, and she was standing there listening intently as if awaiting someone's arrival.

"What has brought you to such a wretched state?" Liu asked.

The girl first expressed her gratitude with a smile; then, unable to restrain her tears, replied, "Unhappy creature that I am! Since you ask me the reason, how can I hide the deep resentment I feel? Listen then! I am the youngest daughter of the Dragon King of Dongting Lake. My parents married me to the second son of the Dragon King of the Jing River; but my husband, devoted to pleasure and led astray by his attendants, treated me more unkindly every day. I complained to his parents, but they were too fond of their son to take my part. When I persisted in complaining, they grew angry and banished me here." Having said this, she broke down and sobbed.

"Dongting Lake is so far away," she went on. "It lies beyond the distant horizon, and I can get no word to my family. My heart is breaking and my eyes are worn out with watching, but there is no one to know my grief or pity me. Since you are going south and will pass near the lake, may I trouble you to take a letter?"

"I have a sense of justice," answered Liu, "and your story makes my blood boil. I only wish I had wings to fly there—why talk of trouble? But the lake is very deep, and I can only walk on land. How am I to convey your message? I fear I may be unable to get through, proving unworthy of your trust and failing in my own sincere wish to help you. Can you tell me how to make the journey?"

"I cannot say how I appreciate your kindness," said the girl, shedding tears. "If ever I receive a reply, I shall repay you even if it costs my life. Before you promised to help me, I dared not tell you how to reach my parents; but actually, to go to the lake is no harder than going to the capital."

Asked for directions, she told him, "South of the lake stands a big orange tree which is the sacred tree of the village. Take off this belt, put on another, and knock on the trunk three times. Someone will come to your call, and if you follow him you will have no difficulty. I have opened my heart to you as well as trusting you with my letter. Please tell my parents what you have heard. On no account fail me!"

Liu promised to do as she said. Then the girl took a letter from her pocket and handed it to him with a bow, all the while looking eastwards and weeping in a way that touched his heart.

When he had put the letter in his wallet, he inquired,

"May I ask why you herd sheep? Do deities also eat cattle?"

"No," she answered. "These are not sheep, but rain-bringers."

"What are they?"

"Thunder, lightning, and the like."

Liu looked at the sheep closely, and saw that they moved proudly with heads held high. They cropped the grass differently too, although they were the same size as ordinary sheep and had the same wool and horns.

"Now that I am going to act as your messenger," he said, "I hope in future, when you get back to the lake, you won't refuse to see me."

"Certainly not!" she exclaimed. "I shall treat you as a dear relative."

Then they bid each other goodbye, and he started east. After a few dozen yards he looked back, but both girl and sheep had disappeared.

That evening he reached the county town and said goodbye to his friend. It took him over a month to get home, and he went without delay to Dongting Lake. He found the orange tree south of the lake, changed his belt, faced the tree and knocked three times. A warrior came out of the water, and bowed to him. "Why have you come here, honourable sir?" he asked.

Without telling him the story, Liu simply answered, "To see your king."

The warrior parted the waves and pointed the way, saying to Liu as he led him down, "Close your eyes. We will be there in no time."

Liu did as he was told, and soon they reached a great palace where he saw clustered towers and pavilions, millions of gates and arches, and all the rare plants and trees of the world. The warrior asked him to wait at the corner of a great hall.

"What place is this?" asked Liu.

"The Palace of the Divine Void."

Looking round, Liu saw that this palace was filled with every precious object known to man. The pillars were of white jade, the steps of jasper; the couches were of coral, the screens of crystal. The emerald lintels were set with cut glass, while the rainbow-coloured beams were inlaid with amber. And the whole created an impression of strange beauty and unfathomable depth which defied description.

The Dragon King was a long time in coming, and Liu asked the warrior, "Where is the Lord of Dongting?"

"His Majesty is in the Dark Pearl Pavilion," was the reply. "He is discussing the Fire Canon with the Sun Priest, but will have finished soon."

"What is the Fire Canon?" Liu wanted to know.

"Our king is a dragon," was the reply, "so water is his element, and with one drop of water he can flood mountains and valleys. The priest is a man, so fire is his element, and with one torch he can burn down a whole palace. Since the properties of the elements differ, they have different effects. As the Sun Priest is expert in the laws of men, our king has asked him over for a talk."

He had barely finished speaking when the palace gate opened, a mist seemed to gather and there appeared a man in purple holding a jasper sceptre. The warrior leaped to attention, crying, "This is our king!" Then he went forward to report Liu's arrival.

The Dragon King looked at Liu and asked, "Are you not of the world of men?"

Liu replied that he was, and bowed. The king greeted him in return and asked him to be seated.

"Our watery kingdom is dark and deep, and I am ignorant," said the Dragon King. "What has brought you, sir, from such a distance?"

"I am of the same district as Your Majesty," replied Liu. "I was born in the south, but have studied in the northwest. Not long ago, after failing in the examination, I was riding by the Jing River when I came upon your daughter herding sheep in the open country. Exposed to wind and rain, she was a pitiful sight. When questioned, she told me she had come to such a pass because of her husband's unkindness and his parents' neglect. I assure you, her tears as she spoke went to my heart. Then she entrusted this letter to me and I promised to deliver it. That is why I am here." He took out the letter and passed it to the king.

After reading the missive, the king covered up his face and wept. "Though I am her old father," he lamented, "I have been like a man blind and deaf, unaware that my child was suffering far away, while you, a stranger, came to her rescue. As long as I live, I shall never forget your kindness." He gave way to weeping, and all the attendants shed tears.

Presently a palace eunuch approached the king, who handed him the letter with orders to tell the women in the inner palace. Soon wailing was heard from within and in alarm the king bade his attendants, "Quickly tell the women not to make so much noise, or the Prince of Qiantang may hear them!"

"Who is this prince?" asked Liu.

"My younger brother," said the Dragon King. "He used to be the Prince of the Qiantang River, but has now retired."

"Why must you keep it from him?"

"Because he is overbold," was the reply. "The nine

years of flood in the time of the ancient sage King Yao was due to one of his rages. Not long ago he quarrelled with the angels in heaven and flooded the five mountains. Thanks to a few good deeds I had to my credit, the heavenly emperor pardoned him; but he has to be kept here. The people of Qiantang are waiting still for his return."

He had scarcely finished when there came a great crash, as if both heaven and earth had been torn asunder. The palace shook and mist seethed as in burst a crimson dragon more than a thousand feet long, dragging after it a jade pillar to which its neck had been fastened by a gold chain. Its eyes were bright as lightning, its tongue red as blood, and it had scarlet scales and a fiery mane. Thunder crashed and lightning flashed around it, then snow and hail fell thick and fast, after which it soared up into the azure sky.

Panic-stricken, Liu had fallen to the ground. But now the king himself helped him up, urging, "Have no fear! All is well."

After a long time, Liu recovered a little. And when calm enough he asked leave to withdraw. "I had better go while I can," he explained. "I couldn't survive another experience like that."

"There's no need to leave," said the king. "That's the way my brother goes, but he won't come back that way. Do stay a little longer." He called for wine, and they drank to pledge their friendship.

Then a soft breeze sprang up, wafting over auspicious clouds. Amid flying pennons and flags and the sound of flutes and pipes, in came thousands of brightly dressed, laughing and chattering girls. Among them was one with beautiful, arched eyebrows who was wearing bright jewels and a gown of the finest gauze. When she drew near, Liu saw that she was the girl who had given him the message. Now she was shedding tears of joy, as she moved through a fragrant red and purple mist to the inner palace.

The king said with a laugh to Liu, "Here comes the prisoner from the Jing River!" He excused himself and went inside, and from the inner palace happy weeping was heard. Then the king came out again to feast with Liu.

Presently a man in purple strode up to stand by the king. He was holding a jasper sceptre and looked vigorous and full of spirit. The king introduced him as the Prince of Qiantang.

Liu stood up to bow, and the prince bowed in return. "My unhappy niece was insulted by that young blackguard," he said. "It was good of you, sir, with your strong sense of justice, to carry the news of her wrongs so far. If not for you, she would have pined away by the Jing River. No words can express our gratitude."

Liu bowed and thanked him. Then the prince told his brother, "I reached the river in one hour, fought there for another hour, and took another hour to come back. On my return journey I flew to high heaven to report to the Heavenly Emperor; and when he knew the injustice done he pardoned me. In fact, he pardoned my past faults as well. But I am thoroughly ashamed that in my indignation I did not stop to say goodbye, upsetting the whole palace and alarming our honourable guest." He bowed again.

"How many did you kill?" asked the king.

"Six hundred thousand."

"Did you destroy any fields?"

"About three hundred miles."

"Where is that scoundrel, her husband?"

"I ate him."

The king looked pained.

"Of course that young blackguard was insufferable," he said. "Still, that was going rather far. It is lucky that the Heavenly Emperor is omniscient and pardoned you because such a great injustice had been done. Otherwise what could I have said in your defence? Don't ever do that again!" The prince bowed once more.

That evening Liu was lodged in the Hall of Frozen Light, and the next day another feast was given at the Emerald Palace. All the royal family gathered there, music was played, and wine and delicacies were served. Then bugles, horns and drums sounded as ten thousand warriors danced with flags, swords and halberds on the right-hand side, while one came forward to announce that this was the triumphal march of the Prince of Qiantang. This spectacular and awe-inspiring display impressed all who saw it.

Then to an accompaniment of gongs and cymbals, stringed and bamboo instruments, a thousand girls dressed in bright silks and decked with jewels danced on the left-hand side, while one came forward to announce that this music was to celebrate the return of the princess. The melodies were poignant and sweet, breathing such grief and longing that all who heard were moved to tears. When the two dances were over, the Dragon King in high good humour made the dancers presents of silk. Then the guests sat down together to feast, and drank to their hearts' content.

When they had drunk their fill, the king rapped on the table and sang:

Wide the earth and grey the sky,
Who can hear a distant cry?
The fox lies snugly in his lair,

But thunderbolts can reach him there.
A true man, who upholds the right,
Restored my daughter to my sight.
Such service how can we requite?

After the king's song ended, the prince made a bow and sang:

Life and death are fixed by fate,
Our princess found a worthless mate.
By River Jing she had to go,
In wind and frost, in rain and snow.
This gentleman her letter bore,
Then we restored her to this shore.
This we'll remember evermore!

After this song, the king and prince stood up and each presented a cup to Liu, who hesitated bashfully before accepting, then quaffed off the wine, returned the cups and sang:

Like a blossom in the rain,
The princess longed for home in vain,
I brought back tidings of her plight,
And all her wrongs were soon set right,
Now we feast, but soon must part,
For home again I needs must start.
Bitter longing fills my heart!

This song of his was greeted by loud applause.

The king brought out a jasper casket of rhinoceros horn which could part the waves, and the prince an amber dish bearing jade that shone at night. They presented these to Liu, who accepted the gifts with thanks. Then the inmates of the palace started piling silk and jewels beside him, until gorgeous materials were heaped up all around. Laughing and chatting with the company, he had not a moment's quiet. Sated at last with wine and pleasure, he excused himself and went back to sleep in the Hall of Frozen Light.

The next day he was feasting again in the Pavilion of Limpid Light when the Prince of Qiantang, heated with wine and lounging on the couch, said insolently, "A hard rock can be smashed but not made to yield, and a gallant man can be killed but not put to shame. I have a proposal to make. If you agree, all will be well between us. If not, we can perish together. How about it?"

"Let me hear your proposal," said Liu.

"As you know, the wife of the Lord of the Jing River is our sovereign's daughter," said the prince. "She is an excellent girl with a fine character, well thought of by all her kinsmen but unlucky enough to have suffered indignities at the hands of that scoundrel. However, that's a thing of the past. We would like to entrust her to you, and become your relatives for ever. Then she who owes you gratitude will belong to you, and we who love her will know she is in good hands. A generous man shouldn't do things by halves. Don't you agree?"

For a moment Liu looked grave. Then he rejoined with a laugh, "I never thought the Prince of Qiantang would have such unworthy ideas. I have heard that once when you crossed the nine continents, you shook the five mountains to give vent to your anger; and I have seen you break the golden chain and drag the jade pillar after you to rescue your niece. I thought there was no one as brave and just as you, who dared risk death to right a wrong, and would sacrifice your life for those you love. These are the true marks of greatness. Yet now, while music is being played and host and guest are in harmony, you try to force me to do your

will in defiance of honour. I would never have expected this of you! If I met you on the angry sea or among dark mountains, with your fins and beard flying and mist and rain all around, though you threatened me with death I should consider you a mere beast and not count it against you. But now you are in human garb. You talk of manners and show a profound understanding of human relationships and the ways of men. You have a nicer sense of propriety than many gallants in the world of men, not to say monsters of the deep. Yet you try to use your strength and temper—while pretending to be drunk—to force me to agree to your proposal. This is hardly right. Although small enough to hide under one of your scales, I am not afraid of your anger. I hope you will reconsider your proposal."

Then the prince apologized. "Brought up in the palace, I was never taught etiquette," he said. "Just now I spoke wildly and offended you—your rebuke was well deserved. Don't let this spoil our friendship." That night they feasted together again as merrily as ever, and Liu and the prince became great friends.

The day after, Liu asked permission to leave. The queen gave another feast for him in the Hall of Hidden Light, which was attended by a great throng of men and women, maids and servants. Shedding tears, the queen said to him, "My daughter owes you so much, we can never repay you. And we are sorry to have to say goodbye." She told the princess to thank him.

"Shall we ever meet again?" asked the queen.

Liu regretted now that he had not agreed to the prince's request. His heart was very heavy. After the feast, when he bid them farewell, the whole palace was filled with sighing, and countless rare jewels were given him as parting gifts.

He left the lake by the way he had come, escorted by a dozen or more attendants who carried his bags to his home before leaving him. He went to a jeweller's at Yangzhou to sell some of the jewels, and though he parted with about one hundredth only he became a multi-millionaire, wealthier by far than all the rich men west of the Huai River.

He married a girl called Zhang, but soon she died. Then he married a girl called Han; but after several months she died as well, and Liu moved to Nanjing.

Loneliness tempted him to marry again, and a go-between told him, "There is a girl called Lu from Fanyang County, whose father, Lu Hao, used to be magistrate of Qingliu. In his later years he studied Taoist philosophy and lived by himself in the wilderness, so that now no one knows where he is. Her mother was named Zheng. The year before last the girl married into the Zhang family at Qinghe, but unfortunately her husband died. Because she is young, intelligent and beautiful, her mother wants to find a good husband for her. Are you interested?"

So Liu married this girl on an auspicious day, and since both families were wealthy, the magnificence of their gifts and equipage impressed the whole city of Nanjing.

Coming home one evening about a month after their marriage, Liu was struck by his wife's resemblance to the Dragon King's daughter, except that she was in better health and more lovely. Accordingly, he told her what had happened.

"I can't believe it," she replied. Then she told him that she was with child, and Liu became more devoted to her than ever.

A month after the child was born, Liu's wife dressed

herself in fine clothes, put on her jewels, and invited all their relatives to the house. Before the assembled company she asked him with a smile, "Don't you remember meeting me before?"

"Once I carried a message for the Dragon King's daughter," he replied. "That is something I have never forgotten."

"I am the Dragon King's daughter," she said. "Wronged by my former husband, I was rescued by you, and I swore to repay your kindness. But when my uncle the prince suggested that we marry, you refused. After our separation we lived in two different spheres, and I had no way of sending word to you. Later my parents wanted to marry me to another river god—that stripling of the Zhuoqin River—but I remained true to you. Although you had forsaken me and there was no hope of seeing you again, I would rather have died than stop loving you. Soon after that, my parents took pity on me and decided to approach you again; but you married girls from the Zhang and Han families, and there was nothing we could do. After those girls had died and you came to live here, my family felt the match was possible. But I never dared hope that one day I might be your wife. I shall be grateful and happy all my life, and die without regret." So saying, she wept.

Presently she went on: "I did not disclose myself to you before, because I knew you did not care for my looks. But I can tell you now that I know you are attached to me. I am not good enough to keep your love, so I'm counting on your fondness for the child to hold you. Before I knew you loved me, I was so anxious and worried! When you took my letter, you smiled at me and said, 'When you go back to the lake, don't refuse to see me!' Did you want us to become husband

and wife in future? Later when my uncle proposed the marriage and you refused him, did you really mean it or were you just offended? Do tell me!"

"It must have been fated," said Liu. "When first I met you by the river, you looked so wronged and pale, my heart bled for you. But I think all I wanted at the time was to pass on your message and right your wrong. When I said I hoped you wouldn't refuse to see me in future, that was just a casual remark with nothing behind it. The prince's attempt to force me into marriage annoyed me because I object to being bullied. Since a sense of justice had motivated my action, I could hardly marry the woman whose husband's death I had caused. As a man of honour I had to do what I thought right. So during our drinking I spoke from my heart, saying only what was just, with no fear of him. Once the time came to leave, however, and I saw the regret in your eyes, I was rather sorry. But after I left the lake, the affairs of this world kept me too occupied to convey my love and gratitude to you. Well, now that you belong to the Lu family and are a woman, I find my former feelings towards you were more than a fleeting passion after all! From now on, I shall love you always."

His wife was deeply moved and replied with tears, "Don't think human beings alone know gratitude. I shall repay your kindness. A dragon lives for ten thousand years, and I shall share my span of life with you. We shall travel freely by land and sea. You can trust me."

"I never thought you could tempt me with immortality!" laughed Liu.

They went to the lake again, where the royal entertainment once more given them beggars description.

Later they lived at Nanhai for forty years. Their mansions, equipage, feasts and clothes were as splendid as those of a prince, and Liu was able to help all his relatives. His perennial youth amazed everybody. During the Kai Yuan period (AD 713-741), when the emperor set his heart on discovering the secret of long life and searched far and wide for alchemists, Liu was given no peace and went back with his wife to the lake. Thus he disappeared from the world for more than ten years. At the end of that period, his younger cousin, Xue Gu, lost his post as magistrate of the capital and was sent to the southeast. On his journey Xue crossed Dongting Lake. It was a clear day and he was looking into the distance when he saw a green mountain emerging from the distant waves. The boatmen shrank back in fear, crying, "There was never any mountain here —it must be a sea monster!"

As they were watching the mountain approach, a painted barge came swiftly towards them and the men on it called Xue's name. One of them told him, "Master Liu sends his greetings." Then Xue understood. Invited to the foot of the mountain, he picked up the skirt of his gown and went quickly ashore. On the mountain were palaces like those on earth, and Liu was standing there with musicians before and bejewelled girls behind him, more splendid than in the world of men. Talking more brilliantly and looking even younger than formerly, he greeted Xue at the steps and took his hand.

"We have not been separated long," he said, "yet your hair is turning grey."

"You are fated to become an immortal and I to become dry bones," retorted Xue with a laugh.

Liu gave him fifty capsules, and said, "Each of these will give you an extra year of life. When you have finished them, come again. Don't stay too long in the world of men, where you must undergo so many hardships." They feasted happily, and then Xue left. Liu was never seen again, but Xue often related this story. And fifty years later, he too vanished from the world.

This tale shows that the principal species of each category* of living creatures possesses supernatural powers—for how otherwise could reptiles assume the virtues of men? The Dragon King of Dongting showed himself truly magnanimous, while the Prince of Qiantang was impetuous and straightforward. Surely their virtues did not appear from nowhere. Liu's cousin, Xue Gu, was the only other human being to penetrate to that watery kingdom, and it is a pity that none of his writings have been preserved. But since this account holds such interest, I have recorded it here.

Written by Li Chaowei
Translated by Gladys Yang

---

*The ancient Chinese divided the animal kingdom into five categories: feathered, furred, hard-shelled, scaly and hairless. The chief species of these categories were phoenix, unicorn, tortoise, dragon and man. From man, the most intelligent of all, these others derived some of their virtues.

The Monk Xuan Zhao

THE monk Xuan Zhao practised Buddhism at White Magpie Ravine on Mount Songshan. He ranked first in the fraternity of monks for his consummate virtues and preached the *Saddharma-pundarika Sutra* a thousand times for the benefit of others. Though in the mountains, his house was always packed with people who came to listen to him preach in spite of bitterly cold and sweltering hot days, going across craggy hills and thick woods to get there.

In the audience for many days running were three strange-looking old men, their eyebrows and hair already white with age, who listened attentively to him. Xuan Zhao wondered to see them. One morning after paying their respects to him they said, "We three students are dragons and have each toiled at our tasks for more than a thousand years. We have learned much from your great power of salvation but have no opportunity to repay you. If your reverence would direct us, we would render our services."

"A drought has continued for a long time in the country," Xuan Zhao said. "The people are suffering from famine. If you could send rain to save those creatures, I should be pleased."

"Summoning clouds and sending rain may be a mere trifle, but it is strictly prohibited. If we do it without orders, it would cause us to be reproved or decapitated. It is a matter of life and death. Yet a ruse occurs to me which will very likely work. Will your reverence comply?"

"Pray tell me it."

"The retired scholar Sun Simiao on Shaoshi Mountain is well-known for his philosophic learning and noble character," said the three old men. "He could certainly snatch us from disaster, and then it could rain in no time."

"I know only that he lives in the mountains. I am ignorant of his conduct. How can he do what you expect?"

"His kindness is infinite, and his valuable medical prescriptions will benefit thousands of generations and have won a reputation for him in the imperial palace. He is virtually divine. If he could say a good word for us, we would be saved. But you have to make him promise first before we send the rain." With this they taught him what to do to rescue them.

Xuan Zhao consented and went to call upon Simiao. Courteously he paid his respects to him and sat there for a while, then said, "Your wise philosophy has inclined you to save others. The standing crops in the fields are being scorched by the burning sun, and the people clamour for food. Now is surely the time for kind philosophy to find a use. I hope you will show mercy to the people and rescue them from starvation."

"Sheer incapacity has made me a recluse in the mountains," replied Simiao. "What power or ability of mine would suffice to succour the people? If I had it, I would not stint it."

"I met three dragons yesterday," said Xuan Zhao. "I

told them to send rain. They said, 'Without orders from God we are forbidden to do so under pain of death. Only a scholar of great deeds and exalted virtues could save us from disaster.' So I have come here to consult you, in the hope that you will consider what to do."

"As long as it is feasible, I will spare no pains to comply."

"After the rain, the three dragons will hide themselves in the pond behind your house to escape punishment. A strange man will come to arrest them, and you must explain and send him away, so that the dragons will be saved."

Simiao consented, and Xuan Zhao left. On the left side of the road he saw the three old men and told them of Simiao's agreement. They promised that it would rain one day and one night over all of a thousand li.

And it did so punctually. The following day Xuan Zhao came to see Simiao. While talking, they saw a strange looking man go straight to the edge of the pond and snarl. At once the water froze, then three otters, two black and one white, climbed out. The man tied them with a red rope, and as he was taking them away, Simiao halted him, saying, "The crime these creatures committed is not expiable, but the order to commit it was given by myself yesterday. This is the truth. I hope you will set them free. Spare them, I beseech you."

The man consented readily and releasing them left with his rope. The three old men took time to express their thanks to Simiao and said that they would repay him.

"Living in the mountains I lack for nothing. You need not repay me."

When they returned to Xuan Zhao, they said that

they would exert their strength on his behalf.

"As I live in the mountains," said Xuan Zhao, " my meals and my cassock are quite sufficient for me. I want for nothing. You need not repay me either."

They pressed him, however, so Xuan Zhao said, "The mountain ahead inconveniently blocks my way in and out. Can you remove it?"

"A mere trifle," they said. "If you do not mind thunder, we will do it at once."

That very night the thunder rumbled and crashed, and by the first light of dawn the mountain before the temple was no more to be seen. The way for several li ahead was smooth as the palm of a hand, whereupon the three old men reappeared, said their thanks and departed.

Most remarkable was Simiao's moral integrity in never asking requital of them.

Translated by Song Shouquan

Liu Guanci

DURING the Da Li period (AD 766-779) of the Tang Dynasty Liu Guanci, a native of Luoyang, went begging in Suzhou, where he met the licentiate Cai Xia, a handsome and bright-looking man, and very sociable, who addressed Guanci as brother and invited him home for roast mutton and wine. While drinking he asked, "What are you travelling over the country for, brother?"

"I'm just begging," Liu Guanci answered.

"Where are you making for? Or are you just wandering from prefecture to prefecture?"

"Just wandering about."

"How much do you want to beg before you give up?" Cai Xia demanded.

"A hundred thousand," was his reply.

"That is a fair sum to obtain by wandering about. You might as well hope to fly away without wings. I grant you, it will take several years. I come from the neighbourhood of Luoyang and am not poor. I had a reason for fleeing my native place and have lost contact with my family for a long time. I should like to ask you please to go there for me. Travelling money and the sum you want you will get in no time. What do you say to it?"

"I should be delighted," said Guanci.

Accordingly Cai Xia gave him the hundred thousand and a letter. He then explained, "Though we have discarded the formalities, we are still on good terms. I come of the scaly breed, and my family lives under a bridge over the River Wei. Close your eyes and knock on the pier of the bridge. You will hear a response and be invited in. When my mother comes out and meets you, ask her to permit you to see my younger sister. Now that we are brothers, you need not stand on ceremony. I have said in my letter that she should come out to greet you. Though young, she is clever. Ask her to make you master of the house and bring you a hundred strings of cash*, and she will not refuse."

Liu Guanci went down to the bridge without delay. Seeing the deep, clear water, he wondered how he would reach his destination. But after some time he decided that the Dragon God would not deceive him and tried closing his eyes and knocking on the bridge. Sure enough a voice answered him. He opened his eyes to see. The bridge and the water had vanished from sight. Before him was an official residence with a vermilion gate and inside it peak beyond peak of buildings and halls. In front of the gate stood men in purple, who asked him his business.

"I come from the prefecture of Wu. Your young master has sent me with a letter," he replied.

His questioner took the letter in. After a while he came out again, saying, "Her Ladyship asks you in."

He complied. The lady looked about forty years of age. She was all in purple and quite charming. Liu

*A string held a thousand cash.

Guanci paid his respects to her, and the lady returned his courtesies.

"My son is off in distant parts. I have not heard of him for ages. It must have been a great trouble for you to come so far with the letter. My son lost favour with his superior in his younger days and left because of the grudge against him. For three years I have received no word from him. You have relieved my anxiety." With this she asked him to be seated.

"Your son treats me as a brother, so his younger sister is mine too. I should see her."

"Yes, so his letter says. She is making her toilet and will be along in a moment."

After a little a maid announced, "The young mistress."

She was about fifteen years of age, a paragon of beauty and understanding. Dropping a curtsey she took a seat beside her mother; then the table was laid with tempting dainties. As they sat down to eat the eyes of the old lady suddenly turned red and fixed on Guanci.

"He has just arrived," said the girl hurriedly. "Let us be courteous. Besides, we rely on him to remove the impending ill fortune, so you must not change your mind." Then she turned to Guanci. "In his letter my brother bids me present you with a hundred strings of cash. Rather than encumber you, I will give you something more portable, if you agree: a vessel of equal value."

"Now that I am his brother, it would not be seemly to take a reward for bringing his letter to you," Guanci returned.

"You are poor and a wandering beggar," the old lady

put in. "This my son has told us in detail. You have been entrusted with the task and must not reject it."

Guanci expressed his gratitude to her, and an exorcism bowl was brought to him. After that they went on eating. For a little the old lady stared at him with her red eyes once more, and spittle ran down from the corners of her mouth.

The girl quickly covered her mouth. "Mother," she said, "my brother assuredly trusts him. You must not do this." Then she turned to Guanci and said, "My mother is having a fit. It is her age. She cannot talk with you now. Pray go out for a moment."

The girl seemed nervous and, bidding the maid take the bowl, followed behind him and handed it to Guanci. "The bowl is from Kashmir, where it was used to fend off disaster. It was brought here in the Tang Dynasty and has been of no use since. You can sell it for one hundred thousand cash, but take no less. My mother is ill and I must attend her, so I will leave you now." So saying she bowed and retired.

Bowl in hand, Guanci went only a few paces before he turned to look. The green water in the river and the bridge over it were there as before. When he looked at the vessel it was an ordinary brass bowl worth no more than three to five cash. He thought he must have been deceived by his dragon sister, but when he was hawking it in the market, one man offered him seven or eight hundred, while another would have paid five hundred. At this he was convinced that the Dragon Goddess had been as good as her word and not tried to fool him. So he took it to the market every day. About a year later a merchant coming from afar was delighted to see it and asked him how much he wanted for it.

"Two hundred strings of cash," was his reply.

"An object should fetch its real value, and this would be worth much more than two hundred strings if it were a treasure of China, but it is not. As things stand, you may own it but never benefit from it. Will you take one hundred strings of cash for it?"

This was what he had expected, and he accepted without bargaining.

"The bowl comes from Kashmir, where it was used to protect the country from disasters," said the merchant. "Since it was lost the country has been ravaged by successive wars. I heard that the son of the Dragon made away with it four years ago. My king will give half his revenues to redeem it. How did you obtain it, sir?"

Guanci told him the whole truth.

"The Guardian Dragon of Kashmir has appealed to the government, and they are looking for it. That is why Cai Xia fled: the officials of the underworld are very strict, and he does not dare surrender himself to be judged there. So he made you carry it to me. His insistence on your meeting his sister was not to cement the relationship between you and him. Considering that the Old Dragon was greedy to devour you, he meant his sister to defend you. Now that the bowl has been brought to light, he will come here too, and all our woes will pass away. In fifty days' time you will see the rivers Cao and Luo rise. When they murmur on a gloomy day, Cai Xia is coming."

"Why in fifty days' time?" Guanci asked.

"I dare not tell you until I've gone across the mountain," he answered.

Guanci made a mental note of his words. When the day arrived, he went there to see. Sure enough the merchant's prediction came true.

Translated by Song Shouquan

Madam Wei

IN Jingzhao lived a woman surnamed Wei, a daughter of a renowned family, who married Meng in Wuchang. At the end of the Da Li period Meng and the scholar Wei, the brother of his wife, were elected at the same time, Wei to be commandant of Yangzi County and Meng to be administrative supervisor of Langzhou. They parted and went to their respective posts.

Madam Wei followed her husband to Shu.* As carriages could not travel the path, she rode on a horse. Suddenly the horse shied at the mouth of a ravine, and she was pitched into an abyss thousands of feet deep. It was too dark to see anything; no one could go down to find her. Her husband Meng and his family wept bitterly. They did not know what to do next. Finally they held a memorial ceremony for her and went away in mourning.

But Madam Wei had in fact fallen unscathed into dried leaves scores of feet thick. At first she could not catch her breath, but after a little she came round. A day later she felt hungry and wrapped some snow in some leaves and ate it. She found a crevice in the rock but did not know how deep it was. She looked up to the hole through which she had dropped. It was the size of

*Present-day Sichuan.

a well. She thought her life had come to an end. All of a sudden a light appeared in a cavern. It grew bigger and bigger then divided into two. As they closed in, they were revealed as the eyes of a dragon. Panic-stricken, she stood against the rock wall. It emerged, more than fifty feet long. At the mouth of the cavern it rose up in the air and flew out. A little later another pair of eyes came into view; it was another dragon. Madam Wei, knowing she might well die, steeled herself, and as the second dragon was going out she pulled herself astride. The dragon did not turn to look at her but leaped out of the cavern and soared into the sky. Afraid to look down, she let it go wherever it liked. Probably half a day had passed, and she reckoned it had covered ten thousand li, when opening her eyes, she saw it was going down. A river and woods came into sight, only forty-odd feet away from her. For fear that she would be plunged into the river, she let herself drop to the thick grass under her. Only after a long while did she come to. She had not eaten for three or four days and was exhausted. As she went languidly along, she met an old fisherman. Taken aback, he did not suppose that she was an earthling.

She asked where she was.

"Yangzi County," was the reply.

She was delighted inwardly, and asked again, "How far is it to the county seat?"

"Twenty li," the fisherman answered.

Madam Wei told him the whole story, and said that she was very hungry and thirsty. Though astonished, he felt for her and fetched her tea and porridge from the boat.

"I suppose Commandant Wei of the county has arrived, has he?" she queried.

"I'm afraid I can't tell you," the fisherman replied.

"I'm his sister. If you'll take me in your boat to the county seat, you'll be rewarded handsomely."

The fisherman consented and took her there. The commandant had arrived quite a few days before. At the gate she had herself announced as thirteenth sister Meng. He did not believe it. "Thirteenth sister followed her husband Meng to Shu. How could she be here so rapidly?"

Madam Wei directed his man to tell him her story. Though surprised, he was not convinced. At last he came out to meet her. Crying, Madam Wei poured forth the hardships she had gone through, until weariness robbed her of words. She was then taken in and tended. Soon her health was entirely restored. Nevertheless, scholar Wei was troubled by doubt, but several days later the bad news came from Shu. Only this dispelled his suspicion. Between sorrow and joy, he rewarded the fisherman with twenty thousand cash then dispatched an attendant to escort his sister to Shu, where Meng was overwhelmed with the same feelings.

Decades later Pei Gang, the cousin of Madam Wei, was still commandant of Gaoan in Hongzhou. It was he who related the story.

Translated by Song Shouquan

Ren Xu

IN the early Jian Zhong period (AD 780-783) of the Tang Dynasty the scholar Ren Xu of Le'an preferred reading to leading a secular existence. He would have liked to spend his whole life deep in the mountains. One day when he was sitting in his study, an old man came to call upon him. He was in yellow, quite elegant and holding a staff in his hand. Ren Xu asked him to be seated and talked with him. After a while he noticed that the man's speech was slurred and that he had a pained look. He seemed to be troubled by something.

"What is worrying you? Why are you looking so dejected?" asked Ren Xu. "Is some sickness at home causing you anxiety?"

"Yes, I have been waiting for your question for a long time," the old man said. "I am not a man, but a dragon. One li to the west is the big pool where I have lived for hundreds of years. I am being harassed by a man, and disaster is almost upon me. Nobody except you can deliver me from death. I came here specially to tell you. Luckily you asked, so I could tell you."

"As a mortal, I know nothing but poetry, history, rites and music. Other skills are quite beyond me. How can I comply?"

"Say only a few words for me. There is no need of other skills."

"Teach me them."

"In two days' time I want you to go to the pool in the morning. At noon there will come a priest from the west. He is my bane. He would drain the pool and kill me. When you see the water drying up, shout loudly, 'Heaven decrees death to any who kill the yellow dragon!' The pool will fill with water. He will try another spell, and you must shout once more. Do this three times and you will have saved me. I will repay you munificently. Hesitate no more."

Ren Xu consented, and the old man thanked him heartily before he left.

Two days later Ren Xu went down the mountains westward. Sure enough he found a big pool there. He sat on the edge of it and waited. At midday there appeared in the west of the sky a wisp of cloud that gradually descended on the pool. From the cloud alighted the priest. He grew bigger and bigger, until he was ten feet tall. On the bank he took charms inscribed with inked characters out of his sleeve and cast them into the water. Soon the water dried up. A yellow dragon was discovered lying on the sandy bottom.

At this Ren Xu shouted loudly, "Heaven decrees death to any who kill the yellow dragon!"

No sooner had he finished speaking than the pool filled with water. Angrily the priest fished out of his sleeve charms inscribed with cinnabar characters and threw them in the pool. The water drained in no time. Ren Xu shouted to Heaven once more, and the pool filled with water a second time. The priest, inflamed with anger, took out of his sleeve a dozen charms inscribed with vermilion characters and threw them all into the air. They changed into fiery clouds and fell into the water, which dried up again. Ren Xu repeated the words, and the pool brimmed once more.

The priest turned to him. "It has taken me ten years to get this dragon to eat. How can you, a Confucian scholar, save the monster?"

With this reproach, he departed, and Ren Xu returned to the mountains too.

That very night he dreamed that the old man came and thanked him saying, "If it had not been for your deliverance, I would have been killed by the priest. I am greatly indebted to you, but grateful words fail me. Let me offer you a pearl, which you will find on the bank of the pool, to express my heartfelt thanks."

Ren Xu went there and sure enough found the pearl in the grass. It was an inch across and so brilliant that he could hardly credit it. When he took it to the market in Guangling, a merchant from afar saw it and remarked, "That pearl is the treasure of a black dragon, such as no mortal has ever obtained."

Ren Xu sold it to the merchant for tens of millions of cash.

Translated by Song Shouquan

The Old Dame by the Fenshui River

AN old dame living by the Fenshui River caught a red carp, the colour of which was quite distinctive from that of other carp. Taking it home, she pitied it in her wonderment, and digging a miniature pond, she drew some water and kept it there. A month later misty clouds were seen swirling up, and the carp flopped about. Shortly it mounted high in the air, and the water in the pond dried up. When night came it returned again. People who had seen it were shocked and considered it a monster. The old dame, afraid that it should make trouble, regretted having brought it home and went to the pond and prayed, "I showed you mercy and let you live on here, but you brought me disaster. Why?"

As soon as she had finished speaking, the carp sprang out of the water and in the wake of a wind-borne cloud dived into the Fenshui River. From the sky dropped a pearl the size of a slingshot, dazzlingly brilliant. Nobody except the old dame dared pick it up.

Five years later her eldest son contracted epilepsy, so badly that no doctor could cure him. She was worried sick. Suddenly she remembered the pearl and sent for a competent physician. Lo and behold, the pearl changed into a pill!

"The red carp left it for me to save my son with in order to repay my kindness," she said.

With that she gave the pill to her son, who took it and soon recovered.

Translated by Song Shouquan

The Rakshas and the Sea Market

MA Ji, whose other name was Longmei, was the son of a merchant. A handsome, unconventional lad, he loved singing and dancing, and his habit of mixing with actors and wearing a silk handkerchief on his head made him look as beautiful as a girl and won him the nickname Handsome. At the age of fourteen he entered the prefectural school, where he was winning quite a name for himself when his father, growing old, decided to retire.

"Son," said the old man, "books cannot fill your belly or put a coat on your back. You had better follow your father's trade."

Ma, accordingly, turned his hand to business.

While on a sea voyage with other traders, Ma was carried off by a typhoon. After several days and nights he reached a city where all the inhabitants were appallingly ugly; yet at the sight of him they exclaimed in horror and fled as if he were a monster. At first Ma was alarmed by their hideous looks, but as soon as he discovered that they were even more afraid of him, he made the most of their fear. Wherever he found them eating or drinking he would rush upon them, and when they scattered in alarm he would regale himself upon all they left.

Later, Ma made his way to a mountain village where the people showed more resemblance to human beings. But they were a ragged, beggarly lot. As he rested under a tree, the villagers gazed at him from a distance, not daring to approach; but realizing after some time that he would not eat them, they began to draw nearer, and Ma addressed them with a smile. Although they spoke different tongues, each side could understand something of what the other said. And when Ma told them that he came from China, the villagers were pleased and spread the news that this stranger was not a cannibal after all. The ugliest of them, however, would turn away after one look at Ma, not daring to draw near. Those who did go up to him had features not entirely different from the Chinese; and as they brought him food and wine Ma asked why they were so afraid of him.

"We were told by our forefathers," they answered, "that nearly nine thousand miles to our west is a country called China inhabited by the most extraordinary looking race. We knew this by hearsay only before; but you have provided proof of it."

Asked the reason for their poverty, they replied: "In our country we value beauty, not literary accomplishments. Our most handsome men are appointed ministers, those coming next are made governors and magistrates, while the third class have noble patrons and receive handsome pensions for the support of their families. But we are considered as freaks at birth, and our parents nearly always abandon us, only keeping us in order to continue the family line."

When Ma inquired the name of their country, they

told him that it was the Great Kingdom of Rakshas and that their capital lay about ten miles to the north. And upon Ma's expressing a desire to be conducted there, they set off with him the next day at cockcrow and reached the city at dawn. The city walls were made of stone as black as ink, with towers and pavilions a hundred feet high. Red stones were used for tiles, and picking up a fragment of one Ma found that it marked his finger-nail just like vermilion. They arrived as the court was rising, in time to see the official equipages. The villagers pointed out the prime minister, and Ma saw that his ears drooped forward in flaps, he had three nostrils, and his eyelashes covered his eyes like a screen. He was followed by some riders who the villagers said were privy councillors. They informed Ma of each man's rank; and, although all the officials were ugly, the lower their rank the less hideous they were.

When Ma turned to leave, the citizens of the capital exclaimed in terror and started flying in all directions, as if he were an ogre. Only when the villagers assured them that there was nothing to be afraid of did these city people dare stand at a distance to watch. By the time he got back, however, there was not a man, woman or child in the country but knew that a man-monster was there; so all the gentry and officials were curious to see him and asked the villagers to fetch him. But whatever house he went to, the gate-keeper would slam the door in his face while men and women alike dared only peep at him through cracks and comment on him in whispers. Not a single one had the courage to invite him in.

Then the villagers told him: "There is a captain of the imperial guard here who was sent abroad on a number of missions by our late king. He has seen so much that he may not be afraid of you."

So they called on the captain, and he was genuinely pleased to meet Ma, treating him as an honoured guest. Ma saw that his host, who looked like a man of ninety, had protruding eyes and a beard like a hedgehog's.

"In my youth," said the captain, "His Majesty sent me to many countries, but never to China. Now at the age of one hundred and twenty, I have been fortunate enough to meet one from your honourable country! I must report this to the king. Living in retirement, I have not been to the court for more than ten years; but I will go there for your sake early tomorrow morning."

He plied Ma with food and drink, showing him every courtesy. After they had drunk a few cups of wine, a dozen girls came in to dance and sing in turn. They looked like devils, but wore white silk turbans and long red dresses which trailed on the ground; and Ma, who could not understand the performance or the songs, found the music weird in the extreme. His host, however, listened appreciatively and asked eventually whether China could boast equally fine music. Receiving an affirmative answer, the old man begged him to sing a few bars. So, beating time on the table, Ma obliged with a tune.

"How strange!" exclaimed the captain, delighted. "It is like the cries of phoenixes or dragons. I have never heard anything resembling this before."

The following day the old man went to the court to recommend Ma to the king, who decided to summon him for an audience. But when two ministers declared that Ma's revolting appearance might shock His Majesty, the king changed his mind. The captain, quite upset, returned to tell Ma of the failure of his mission.

One day, after Ma had stayed with the captain for some time, under the influence of wine he smeared his face with coal dust to perform a sword dance in the role of Zhang Fei*.

"You must appear before the prime minister with your face painted like that," urged the captain, who admired this disguise immensely. "He is sure to patronize you, and will certainly procure you a big salary."

"It is all very well to disguise oneself in fun," protested Ma with a laugh. "But how can I play the hypocrite for the sake of personal gain?"

He gave in, however, when his host insisted.

Then the captain invited a number of high officials to a banquet, and bade Ma paint his face in readiness. When the guests arrived and Ma was called out to meet them, they were all amazed.

"How strange!" they cried. "He used to be so ugly; but now he is quite handsome."

Drinking together, they were soon on the best of terms; and when Ma danced and sang country tunes, they were delighted. The very next day they recommended him to the king, who summoned him to court to question him about the government of China. And his diplomatic answers pleased the king so much that a feast was held in Ma's honour in the pleasure palace.

"I hear that you are skilled in music," said the king as they were drinking. "Will you perform for me?"

Ma immediately rose to dance and sing vulgar tunes, wearing a white turban in imitation of the girls; and

---

*A famous general in the period of the Three Kingdoms (AD 220-280). He is represented on the traditional stage as a man with a dark face and long whiskers.

the king was so amused that he promptly appointed him a privy councillor, thereafter dining with him frequently and showing him extraordinary favour.

As time went on, however, the other officials realized that Ma's face was painted. Wherever he went, people would whisper behind his back or treat him coldly; and such isolation made him uneasy. He addressed a memorial to the throne, requesting permission to retire; but the king refused, granting him only three months' leave. Ma then went back in a carriage loaded with gold and jewels to the mountain village, where the villagers welcomed him on their knees; and, amid thunderous applause, he distributed his wealth among his old friends.

"We are humble people," they said, "yet Your Grace has treated us so kindly! When we go to the Sea Market, we shall look for some precious objects to repay you."

Ma asked where this market was.

"It is a market in the middle of the ocean," they told him, "where mermaids from all the seas bring their jewels and merchants from all the twelve countries around come to trade. Deities frolic there among the coloured clouds and tossing waves; but rich men and high officials will not risk the journey, commissioning us to buy treasures for them instead. The time for the market is at hand."

"How do you know the date?" demanded Ma.

They explained that red birds flew over the ocean seven days before the market; but when Ma asked them when they were going to start, and whether he might go with them, the villagers begged him not to take such a risk.

"I am a sailor," protested Ma. "The wind and waves hold no fears for me."

Soon after this, people came with money to buy goods; then the villagers loaded their wares and boarded a vessel capable of carrying several dozen men. This was a flat-bottomed boat surrounded by a high railing; and with ten men at the oars it cut through the water like an arrow. After a voyage of three days they could make out in the distance, between the moving clouds and water, pavilions rising one behind the other and busy traffic of trading junks. By and by they came to a city, which had walls made of bricks as long as a man's body, and a citadel towering to the sky. Here they moored their boat and went ashore to inspect the treasure displayed in the market precious stones which dazzled the eye, seldom seen in the world of men.

Then a young man rode up, and all the market people hastened to make way for him, crying that this was the Third Prince of Dongyang. The prince's eye fell on Ma as he passed, and he exclaimed:

"This stranger is not from these parts!"

Some of his outriders came to ask Ma where he hailed from; and Ma, bowing at the roadside, told them.

"A kind fate has favoured us with your visit!" cried the prince with a smile. He gave Ma a horse and bade him ride with them out of the West Gate. Upon reaching the shore, their steeds neighed and leapt into the waves; but as Ma cried out in dread the sea parted to form a wall of water on either side; and presently a palace came into sight. It had rafters of tortoise-shell and tiles of fish scales, while its dazzling walls of bright crystal reflected all around. Here they dismounted, and

Ma was led into the presence of the Dragon King who was seated on his throne.

"In the market I came across a talented man from China," the prince reported. "I have brought him here to Your Majesty."

Ma stepped forward to bow to the ground.

"You are a great scholar, sir," said the Dragon King, "not inferior to Qu Yuan, Song Yu and other poets of old. May I ask you to compose a poem on our Sea Market? Pray do not refuse."

Having bowed his agreement, Ma was given a crystal inkstone, dragon's beard brush, paper as white as snow, and ink as fragrant as orchids. Without hesitation he dashed off over one thousand characters which he presented to the Dragon King, who marked the rhythm with one hand as he read the poem.

"Your genius sheds glory on our watery kingdom, sir," said the king.

He then summoned all his dragon kinsmen to feast at the Palace of Rosy Clouds, and, when the wine had circulated freely, raising a goblet in one hand he said to Ma: "My beloved daughter is still unmarried. I would like to entrust her to you, if you have no objection."

Ma rose, blushing, and stammered out his thanks. At once the Dragon King gave an order to his attendants, and presently palace maids led in the princess whose jade pendants tinkled as she walked. Trumpets and drums sounded for the wedding ceremony, and Ma, stealing a look at his bride, found her divinely beautiful. After the ceremony the princess left the hall, and, the feast at an end, two maids holding painted candles led Ma into the inner palace. There the princess was sitting, magnificently arrayed. The bridal bed was of coral, studded with jewels, the curtains were adorned with coloured feathers and decked with huge pearls, and the bedding was soft and scented.

The next morning at dawn, when girl attendants entered to offer their services, Ma got up and went to thank the king. He was duly installed as the royal son-in-law and appointed an official; copies of his poem were dispatched to all the seas, and the dragon rulers of the different oceans sent special envoys to convey their congratulations to the king and invite Ma to feast with them. Then, in embroidered robes and riding on a green-horned dragon, he sallied forth with a magnificent equipage, accompanied by dozens of knights on horseback who carried carved bows and white staffs. They formed a glittering cavalcade, with musicians on horseback and in chariots playing harps and jade flutes. This in three days Ma passed through the different seas, and his fame spread throughout the marine world.

In the palace grew a jade tree, so large that a man could barely encircle it with his arms. The trunk was as transparent as glass and pale yellow in the centre; the branches were slighter than a human arm; and the jasper leaves, little thicker than a coin, cast a fine checkered shade. Ma and his bride often recited poems under this tree, which bore a profusion of blossoms like gardenias. Whenever a petal fell it made a tinkling sound, and picked up proved to be as lovely and bright as carved red agate. Often a strange bird would come to sing here. Its feathers were gold and green, its tail longer than its entire body, and its flute-like voice so clear and plaintive that none who heard it could fail to be moved. Whenever Ma listened to its song, he was carried back in spirit to his native land.

"I have been away from my home and my beloved parents for three years," he told the princess. "The thought of this makes tears well to my eyes and perspiration start out on my back. Will you accompany me home?"

"An immortal must not live like a mortal," she replied. "I cannot go with you, but neither would I let the love of husband and wife stand in the way of your love for your parents. Let us consider this again later."

Hearing this, Ma could not refrain from tears, and the princess sighed.

"It is clear that you cannot have both wife and parents," she said.

Next day, when Ma returned to the palace from an outing, the Dragon King addressed him.

"I hear that you are longing for your home," he said. "Would you like to leave tomorrow?"

Ma thanked the king earnestly.

"Your servant came here as a stranger," he said, "yet you have conferred such honours upon me that I am overwhelmed with gratitude. I shall go to pay my family a short visit, but I hope to return again."

That evening when the princess prepared a parting feast, Ma spoke once more of his proposed return.

"Ah, no," said she. "We can never meet again."

Ma, hearing this, was overcome with grief.

"To go back to your parents shows true filial piety," the princess assured him. "Fate holds endless encounters and separations, and a hundred years pass like a single day; then why should we give way to tears like children? I mean to remain true to you, and I am sure you will be faithful to me. Loving each other in far distant places, we can still be one in spirit: there is no need to remain together morning and night. If you break this pledge, your next marriage will be unlucky; but if you need someone to look after you, you can take a maid as your concubine. I have something to ask you, too. I am now with child, and I would like you to choose a name for it."

"If it is a girl," said Ma, "call her Dragon Palace. If a boy, Happy Sea."

Then the princess asked him for a token, and he gave her a pair of red cornelian lilies he had obtained in the land of the Rakshas.

"Three years from now, on the eighth day of the fourth moon," she charged him, "sail into the south sea and I shall give you your child." Then she handed him a fish-scale bag filled with jewels, saying, "Keep this well. It will support your family for generations."

At dawn the Dragon King held a farewell feast for Ma and bestowed many other gifts on him, after which Ma bid them all adieu and left the palace, escorted by the princess in a carriage drawn by white rams. But as soon as he reached the ocean's shore and dismounted the princess said farewell and turned swiftly away, the salt waves closing over her as she disappeared. Then Ma returned home.

Everybody believed that Ma had been lost at sea, so his family was amazed at his return. His parents were well, but his wife had married again; and Ma realized that when the dragon princess had spoken of keeping faith, she must have known this. His father urged him to marry another wife, but he refused, taking only a concubine. He kept in mind the date, and three years later sailed south again until he saw two children on the ocean's bosom, gambolling and frolicking upon the waves. As he drew near and leant over them, one child seized his arm with a laugh and leapt on to his knee, while the other cried out as if to reproach him for neglecting it. When he had pulled the second child aboard too, he saw that one was a boy and the other a girl. They were beautiful children. Fastened to their coloured hats were his red cornelian lilies, and on the boy's back he found an embroidered bag containing the following letter:

I know that your parents are well. Three years have slipped quickly away while we have been separated by the ocean, with no bluebird to carry our messages. I long for you in my dreams, gazing in grief at the azure sky. Yet even the goddess of the moon pines in loneliness under the cassia tree, and the Weaving Maid grieves as she watches the Milky Way which separates her from her love. Why should I alone enjoy wedded happiness? This thought makes me smile at my tears. Two months after you left I gave birth to twins, who can now prattle and laugh in my lap, and hunt for dates and pears. Since they can manage without a mother now, I am sending them to you; and you will know them by the red cornelian lilies which you gave me. When you take them on your knee, you may imagine that I am beside you. It comforts me to know that you have kept faith; and I too shall remain true to you until death. I no longer rouge or powder my face or darken my eyebrows before the mirror. You are the wanderer and I the loving wife at home; but even though we cannot be together, we remain husband and wife. I feel

it is wrong, though, that your parents should have their grandchildren without meeting their daughter-in-law; so next year when your mother leaves the world, I shall come to the burial and pay my respects. After that, if all goes well with Dragon Palace it may be possible to meet again; and if Happy Sea remains well, a path may be found for a visit. Please take good care of yourself. This letter cannot express all that I want to say.

Ma read and reread this letter, weeping, until the two children put their arms around his neck and said: "Father! Can we go home?"

Pierced to the heart, he fondled them, asking: "Where is our home?"

The children whimpered, and cried for their mother. And Ma gazed at the wild expanse of ocean stretching boundless to the horizon; but no princess appeared, nor any road through the misty waves. There was nothing for it but to take the children home.

Knowing now that his mother's death was near, Ma made everything ready for her funeral, and planted a hundred pine trees in the ancestral graveyard. The next year, when his mother died and the interment took place, a woman appeared beside the grave in deep mourning. As they gazed at her in wonder, a wind sprang up, thunder crashed and rain poured down, and the woman disappeared. But many of the pine trees planted by Ma, which had withered, revived after this rain.

When Happy Sea grew bigger, he still missed his mother; and once he disappeared suddenly into the sea, returning only several days later. But Dragon Palace, being a girl, could not leave home; and she often wept in her room. One day the sky grew dark, and the dragon princess entered Ma's house to comfort her daughter.

"You will have your own home soon," she said. "Don't cry, child."

She gave the girl as her dowry a tree of coral eight feet high, a packet of Baroos camphor, a hundred pearls and two gold boxes set with precious stones. When Ma heard of her coming, he rushed in and took her hands, weeping. But with a clap of thunder the princess vanished.

The recorder of these marvels comments: Men must put on false, ugly faces to please their superiors—such is the hypocritical way of the world. The foul and hideous are prized the world over. Something of which you feel a little ashamed may win praise; while something of which you feel exceedingly ashamed may win much higher praise. But any man who dares to reveal his true self in public is almost certain to shock the multitude and make them shun him. Where, indeed, can that fool of Lingyang* take his priceless jade to weep? Alas! I shall seek my fortune in castles in the clouds and mirages of the sea.

Written by Pu Songling
Translated by Gladys Yang

---

*A man of Lingyang presented a piece of uncut jade to the King of Chu in the Spring and Autumn period (770-476 BC); but the king, not recognizing its value, chopped off the donor's feet in anger.

The Princess of the West Lake

THE young man Chen Bijiao, styled Mingyun, a native of Yan and afflicted by poverty, served the deputy general Jia Wan as a scribe. When their junk was moored on Dongting Lake, a Yangtze alligator rose to the surface of the water. Jia shot an arrow and hit it in the back. At this moment a fish seized it by the tail and would not let go, so that the Yangtze alligator was captured and tied to the mast. On the verge of death its flaring snout seemed to beg Chen to come to its rescue. He was moved and entreated Jia to release it. After dabbing some herb powder on its wound, he let it go. It bobbed in the water for a little before disappearing.

Over a year later the young man went north, and passing through the lake his boat was capsized by a gale. Luckily he caught hold of a bamboo basket and drifted a whole night until brought up by a log, whence he clambered up the bank, only to find a body approaching. It was his page boy. He dragged him out of the water on the verge of death. Grief robbing him of all resource, he sat by the boy to recuperate. Before him were small hills covered with emerald green and the slender verdant branches of weeping willows waving in the breeze. There was not a soul to be seen, nobody of whom to inquire the way. Frustrated, he lay there from dawn till mid-morning, when the limbs of the page boy began to move slightly. Delighted, he set to and chafed him, and he soon came to and brought up gallons of water. They aired their clothes on rocks, where they dried out by noon, and they put them on. By then also their empty stomachs were rumbling; they were mightily hungry. They pressed on up the hill in the hope of finding a village ahead. Halfway up it they heard the whistling of an arrow. Just as they were wondering what it was, they saw two young women on horseback gallop over the ridge. Round their heads were red silk bands, and pheasants' tail feathers were stuck into their coiled hair. They were clad in purple jackets with close-fitting sleeves, and green sashes encircled their waists. In one hand they held slingshot and on the other wore archers' wristguards. Behind them came dozens of mounted women hunting in the brushwood. They were in the same dress.

Chen did not dare proceed, and when a man came running in his direction who seemed to be a groom, he asked him who the women were.

"It's the princess of the West Lake hunting in the mountains," the man replied.

Chen told him who he was and that he was hungry. The groom undid his pack and gave him some food, warning him, "Stand aside; it is death to obstruct them."

Panic-stricken, he hurried down from the mountains. In the thick woods he dimly discerned halls. There must be a monastery here, he thought. Nearing it, he made out a white wall, running through which was a stream. The vermilion gate was ajar, and through it he could see a stone bridge. He peeped in. Inside were high terraces and buildings. Thinking he must be in the royal park or that of a noble family, he hesitantly went in and found creepers blocking his way and a sweet smell greeting him. Beyond a winding railing was a courtyard lined with weeping willows so tall they touched the vermilion eaves. Thrushes twittered, and flower petals flew about. The breeze from the bottom of the garden sent the elm pods dropping. He felt a delightful ease, as if he had come into some fairyland. Passing a little bower, he saw a swing, its top flush with the clouds. But the ropes attached to it were dangled loose; nobody was playing on it. He suspected the ladies' appartments must be near by and dared go no further. Suddenly he heard the clatter of hoofs and female laughter. He and his page boy hid amid the shrubs. Gradually the laughter grew nearer, until he heard one voice saying, "We were not in the mood today. It was a poor bag."

"But for the wildgoose Her Highness shot down, I would have worked my horse to no purpose," said another.

Then a girl surrounded by several maids came up to the bower and took a seat. A cloak over her shoulders and her hair uncombed, she looked not more than fifteen. Her waist was so slim that it seemed unable to brave the wind. It would have been no exaggeration to compare her to a tender bud or a delicate jade. The maids in their rich colours brought her a cup of fragrant tea and some incense. After a while she rose to her feet and went down the steps.

"Is Your Highness too tired with riding," asked one of the maids, "to have a swing just yet?"

The princess smiled her denial. Some of the maids set to and supported her shoulders while others held her arms, lifted up her skirt, took off her slippers and helped her on to the swing. She put out her white arms and donned another pair of shoes. Like a swallow in flight, she arced through the air, and then they helped her down.

"Your Highness really is an immortal," remarked the maids as they left joyfully.

Spying on them for such a long time had enlivened and encouraged him. When everything was still again, he went to the swing and paced up and down around it. Pondering, he caught sight of a red handkerchief under the railing. He knew that it had been left behind by one of the maids. Putting it into his sleeve, he went into the bower. He saw a writing brush and inkstone on a stand and wrote a poem on the handkerchief:

> "Who here amused herself in style so high?
> Some goddess, sure, strewed flowers as she passed by.
> Moon Palace maids cast her a jealous eye
> And credit not her shoes have trod the sky."

After writing this he read it aloud and was about to return to the path, but found that the doors along the way had been bolted. At his wits' end he turned back towards the halls, pavilions and terraces. Finally he saw a girl approaching.

"What are you doing here?" she exclaimed.

"Attempting to leave," he said bowing. "Pray help me. I have lost my way."

"Have you picked up a red handkerchief?"

"Yes, and sullied it. What do you think?" With this he produced it.

"You are as good as dead," cried the girl, astounded.

"The princess always carries it. All these stains! What ever shall we do?"

Filled with consternation, he besought her to deliver him from this disaster.

"It was unforgivable of you to steal a glance into the palaces, but your being so young and decorous inclines me to rescue you. Nonetheless, you have committed a sin, and I shall be hard put to it." So saying she hurried away with the handkerchief.

In fear and trembling Chen regretted that he had no wings. He could do nothing but present his neck to the sword.

After a long time the girl returned. "Congratulations!" she said. "I think you will live. Her Highness looked at the handkerchief three or four times and then smiled instead of flaring up. You could well be released. But wait patiently and be sure not to go climbing up trees and over walls. If you are caught at that, all is lost."

The sun was setting, and he was still not sure what would become of him. He was famished too. Before long, however, the girl came back with a lantern in her hand and a maidservant following behind. The latter presented him with wine and food. Chen was impatient to know what had passed.

"I asked her, 'What about the young man in the garden? If you mean to pardon him, let him go. Otherwise he'll die of starvation,'" said the girl. "After giving it a thought, Her Highness retorted, 'Where do you mean him to go at night?' So she sent the maidservant to you with food, which at any rate is not an evil omen."

He passed a restless night. Half the morning had

passed when the girl brought him food again. He besought her to put in a good word for him.

"Her Highness has not told us whether to kill or release you yet. We are servants and dare not press her."

At sunset when he was looking forward to fresh information, the girl hurried in. "Alas!" she said. "Some meddler has informed the queen. She read the poem on the handkerchief and roundly cursed the writer. Disaster is imminent, I think!"

Chen's face turned pale with distress. He was down on his knees begging for assistance when they heard voices clamouring for his arrest. The girl motioned to him to lie low. Several women, one with a rope in her hand, rushed in. Among them was a maidservant, who looked round carefully.

"Arrest whom?" she asked. "Mr Chen?" She stopped the woman with the rope. "Do nothing before Queen Bai arrives." Then she turned and left. Before long she came back announcing, "Her Majesty will see Mr Chen."

In fear and trepidation he complied. Passing dozens of doors he reached a palace hung with an emerald-green door curtain flanked with silver loops. A pretty girl lifted the curtain and announced him. There before him was a beauty in a brilliant robe. He prostrated himself before her in a kowtow. "Your subject, lady, alone and from afar. Spare me, I beseech you."

The queen sprang to her feet and came towards him. "But for your help, sir," she said, "I would not be alive today. My maids offended you in their ignorance. I scarcely know how to atone."

With that she commanded a sumptuous dinner to be

served in his honour. He drank from a chased cup, like one lost in a fog.

"I am grateful to you for saving my life and will repay you. My daughter is highly honoured by the poem you wrote on her handkerchief. You are surely fated for one another, and this very evening she shall attend you."

This, being beyond his expectations, completely bewildered him.

At dusk a maidservant came saying, "Her Highness' toilet is completed."

Presently Chen was led into a chamber, where flutes and pipes sounded. The steps were covered with woollen carpets. On the railings outside and inside hallway and sideroom were lanterns and candles. Attended by bevies of pretty girls, the princess and Chen bowed to each other and were married. The halls were filled with the scent of musk and orchids, and within the curtain Chen and the princess gave themselves over to love.

"I am a stranger here and unacquainted with your ways," he said. "I am lucky to have escaped death for sullying your precious handkerchief. I never thought that I would marry you."

"My mother," said the princess, "is the consort of the lord of the lake and daughter to the king of the Yangjiang River. Once, swimming home to visit her parents, she was hit by an arrow. It was you who saved her and gave her the herb powder for her wound. The whole family is much obliged to you and has never forgotten your kindness. I hope you will not be suspicious of such weird folk as us. I have learned the secret of longevity from the Dragon Lord. It shall be for both of us."

Only then did Chen realize that she was an immortal. "How did the maid recognize me?" he asked.

"She was the fish that held the tail of the Yangtze alligator in Dongting Lake that day," the princess answered.

"But if you did not want to kill me, you could have detained and then let me go. Why did you not?"

"I loved what I saw in you," she said with a smile, "but I was not my own mistress. I could have tossed about all night without anyone taking any notice."

"Ah, my Bao Shu*! Who brought me the food?"

"Anian, another favourite of mine."

"How shall I thank her?"

"Let her serve you some day. But there will be plenty of time to see to her needs later."

"Where is the king now?"

"Still with the saint Guan Yu crushing the rebel Chi You."

After some days without news of his family, he began to worry and sent his page boy on ahead with a letter to report his safety. Because they had been informed that the boat had capsized in Dongting Lake, his wife and children had been in mourning over a year. Only when his page boy arrived did they learn that he was not dead. Then for half a year correspondence ceased, and they feared that he had drifted off and would not return, when he returned out of the blue, his bags full of precious gems and his fur coat and horse sleekly groomed.

He became a millionaire, generous in word and countenance, and even the most aristocratic families

---

*Bao Shuya, a minister of the State of Qi in the Spring and Autumn period. He was a noted judge of character.

could not rival him in wealth. Over the next eight years he had five children. He gave dinner parties every day as sumptuous as those in the imperial palace and was quite frank when asked how he had come by it all.

A friend of his boyhood, Liang Zijun, had travelled in the south for ten years as an official career and was going via Dongting Lake when he saw a pleasure boat decorated with engraved balustrades and vermilion windows sailing on it. Melodious song accompanied by flutes and pipes rippled from the craft over the sluggish water, and from time to time a beautiful woman pushed open a window to look out, revealing a young man within, bare-headed and cross-legged, being caressed by a pretty girl. He must be a high-ranking official, Liang supposed, except that there was nothing like a retinue about him. He had gazed at him for a little when he realized it was Chen Mingyun. On the spur of the moment Liang leaned over the railing and hailed him. Hearing the call, he had the pleasure boat drop anchor and came out on to the bow to invite Liang aboard, where he saw a table strewn with leftovers. The air smelt of wine. Chen ordered all cleared away, and some lovely maids brought in wine, tea and the most exotic game and seafood Liang had ever seen.

"It is only ten years since we saw each other last. How have you become so rich?" he asked, surprised.

"Was I so poor a scholar that you thought I would never rise in the world?" Chen protested with a smile.

"Who was that drinking with you just now?" Liang inquired further.

"Just my poor wife," Chen replied.

"Where are you going with your family?" Liang wondered.

"West," was his reply.

To forestall another question, Chen had his maids sing while they drank. As soon as the order was out there was a deafening crash of thunder, which with the voices and pipes drowned their voices. At sight of the pretty girls standing before him Liang feigned drunkenness and shouted, "Mingyun, will you have them pleasure me?"

Chen laughed. "You are drunk. But I can give you something that will buy you a lovely concubine." With this he told his maid to present him with a pearl. "Lu Zhu* will not be far to seek. Know by this that I am not a miser. And now," he added dismissively, "a trifle of business must curtail the pleasure of your company."

He saw Liang back to his own boat, weighed anchor and left.

When Liang returned home and called on Chen's family, he found him drinking with his friends. "I saw you on Dongting Lake yesterday," he said, amazed. "How have you come back so speedily?"

"I was never there," Chen replied.

Liang related what he had seen on the lake, which surprised the whole table.

"You are surely mistaken, sir," Chen smiled. "How could I have split myself in two?"

They wondered but were perplexed by this answer.

Chen died at the age of eighty-one. When they lifted the coffin, the bearers thought it very light. Opening it, they found it empty.

The bamboo basket that did not sink (*appends the*

---

*A beautiful concubine of Shi Chong (AD 249-300).

chronicler of these wonders) and Chen's poem on the handkerchief must have been divinely inspired. What is more important is that they were imbued with the spirit of sympathy. It is inexplicable, however, that he could have enjoyed the simultaneous companionship of his concubines in the palace and elsewhere as well as that of his wife at home. There have been those who wished not only for a pretty young wife, lovely concubines and promising children but also for immortality, yet they achieved only half of their wishes. Is it possible that the Lord of Fenyang and Jilun* are also numbered among the immortals?

Written by Pu Songling
Translated by Song Shouquan

*Guo and Shi Ziyi, famous for their numerous concubines and offspring and fabulous wealth.

Legend of the Four Dragons

ONCE upon a time, there were no rivers and lakes on earth, but only the Eastern Sea, in which lived four dragons: the Long Dragon, the Yellow Dragon, the Black Dragon and the Pearl Dragon.

One day the four dragons flew from the sea into the sky. They soared and dived, playing at hide-and-seek in the clouds.

"Come over here quickly!" the Pearl Dragon cried out suddenly.

"What's up?" asked the other three, looking down in the direction where the Pearl Dragon pointed. On the earth they saw many people putting out fruits and cakes, and burning incense sticks. They were praying! A white-haired woman, kneeling on the ground with a thin boy on her back, murmured:

"Please send rain quickly, God of Heaven,
To give our children rice to eat...."

For there had been no rain for a long time. The crops withered, the grass turned yellow and fields cracked under the scorching sun.

"How poor the people are!" said the Yellow Dragon. "And they will die if it doesn't rain soon."

The Long Dragon nodded. Then he suggested, "Let's go and beg the Jade Emperor for rain."

So saying, he leapt into the clouds. The others followed closely and flew towards the Heavenly Palace.

Being in charge of all the affairs in heaven, on earth and in the sea, the Jade Emperor was very powerful. He was not pleased to see the dragons rushing in. "Why do you come here instead of staying in the sea and behaving yourselves?"

The Long Dragon stepped forward and said, "The crops on earth are withering and dying, Your Majesty. I beg you to send rain down quickly!"

"All right. You go back first, I'll send some rain down tomorrow." The Jade Emperor pretended to agree while listening to the songs of the fairies.

"Thanks, Your Majesty!" The four dragons went happily back.

But ten days passed, and not a drop of rain came down.

The people suffered more, some eating bark, some grass roots, some forced to eat white clay when they ran out of bark and grass roots.

Seeing all this, the four dragons felt very sorry, for they knew the Jade Emperor only cared about pleasure, and never took the people to heart. They could only rely on themselves to relieve the people of their miseries. But how to do it?

Seeing the vast sea, the Long Dragon said that he had an idea.

"What is it? Out with it, quickly!" the other three demanded.

"Look, is there not plenty of water in the sea where we live? We should scoop it up and spray it towards the sky. The water will be like rain drops and come down to save the people and their crops."

"Good idea!" The others clapped their hands.

"But," said the Long Dragon after thinking a bit, "we will be blamed if the Jade Emperor learns of this."

"I will do anything to save the people," the Yellow Dragon said resolutely.

"Let's begin. We will never regret it." The Black Dragon and the Pearl Dragon were not to be outdone.

They flew to the sea, scooped up water in their mouths, and then flew back into the sky, where they sprayed the water out over the earth. The four dragons flew back and forth, making the sky dark all around. Before long the sea water became rain pouring down from the sky.

"It's raining! It's raining!"

"The crops will be saved!"

The people cried and leaped with joy. On the ground the wheat stalks raised their heads and the sorghum stalks straightened up.

The god of the sea discovered these events and reported to the Jade Emperor.

"How dare the four dragons bring rain without my permission!" The Jade Emperor was enraged, and ordered the heavenly generals and their troops to arrest the four dragons. Being far outnumbered, the four dragons could not defend themselves, and they were soon arrested and brought back to the heavenly palace.

"Go and get four mountains to lay upon them so that they can never escape!" The Jade Emperor ordered the Mountain God.

The Mountain God used his magic power to make four mountains fly there, whistling in the wind from afar, and pressed them down upon the four dragons.

Imprisoned as they were, they never regretted their actions. Determined to do good for the people forever, they turned themselves into four rivers, which flowed past high mountains and deep valleys, crossing the land from the west to the east and finally emptying into the sea. And so China's four great rivers were formed—the Heilongjiang (Black Dragon) in the far north, the Huanghe (Yellow River) in central China, the Changjiang (Yangtze, or Long River) farther south, and the Zhujiang (Pearl) in the very far south.

Compiled by Zhang Chaodong
Translated by Wu Ling

Dragon Dance at Lantern Festival Time

WHEN the Jade Emperor had his birthday party, all the gods and goddesses came to congratulate him.

The banquet lasted three days and three nights. Little Golden Dragon got tired of it, so he came out to take a break. Suddenly, he heard weeping from down below, so he descended to the world of men, transformed himself into a human being, and spoke to a bitterly weeping girl.

The girl lifted her head and saw a fair, plump boy standing in front of her. "There has not been a single drop of rain for three years," she said through her tears. "The crops have withered, and people have to eat grass roots and bark." She took him to a pit, and pointed at a pile of earth stained with blood. "In order to give the people of the village water to drink, my grandfather told them to drain water from our family's well. But it wasn't enough. My grandfather dug a well day and night. Although he dug about a dozen metres down, there was no water at all. He was so thirsty, hungry and tired that he died of anger...."

Her sad story moved Little Golden Dragon to tears. With a stamp of his foot, he turned into white smoke and went back to the heavenly palace.

The girl saw a pool of clear water appear, with a

print of five claws, at the bottom of the pit at the place where he had stamped his foot. She told the villagers to drink the sweet water, and then cried loudly into the sky, "Thank you for the water, sacred dragon! But a pool of water can't save our crops. Please send us some heavy rain!"

Hearing the people's pleas, Little Golden Dragon flew back to Lingxiao Hall, where the gods had left the banquet with full bellies.

Little Golden Dragon found the Dragon King in the Eastern Sea, and told him of the people's requests. "How can I send rain down without the Jade Emperor's orders?" the drunken Dragon King protested between hiccups. Then Little Golden Dragon went directly to the Jade Emperor, but was stopped by the heavenly guards on duty at the gate. "The Jade Emperor has had too much to drink. Come again tomorrow!"

"One day in heaven equals one year in the world of men," the young dragon thought. "The drought has already lasted for three years. How can people wait another year?" Then he had an idea and went to Thunder God and Lightning Goddess. "Do a good deed, Thunder God and Lightning Goddess!" he pleaded. "Just give off a few thunder claps and lightning flashes, even though there is no rain."

Then he went to Uncle Wind and Aunt Cloud, and said, "Have mercy, Uncle Wind and Aunt Cloud. Disperse a few clouds and blow a gust of wind so that the people can get cool, even if there is no rain."

Soon the sky grew cloudy, a fierce wind blew, thunder roared and lightning flashed. Then Little Golden Dragon rushed to the dragon palace and shouted into the ear of the Dragon King, "The Jade Emperor has ordered you to send rain, but you still sleep. Get up, quickly! Do you dare to violate heavenly law?"

Still in a drunken stupor, the Dragon King heard the sound of wind and thunders, and hurriedly snatched up the rain bottle and poured the water down.

Seeing the lucky rain, people happily thanked Little Golden Dragon.

Soon the Jade Emperor heard the news. Flying into a rage, he summoned all the gods and expressed his intent to have Little Golden Dragon killed.

Thunder God and Lightning Goddess sympathized with the dragon and pleaded for his life. Uncle Wind and Aunt Cloud secretly told the news to the people, who got angry, beating drums and gongs and lighting firecrackers to show their indignation. The Jade Emperor then ordered the dragon to be driven down to earth and burned by the people.

But the people could not bear to do it. After discussing the situation, they loaded gun powder into bamboo tubes to make fireworks. So when they pretended to burn the dragon, sparks flew off in every direction, and flames seemed to roar high. But actually the dragon did not feel the least pain.

From then on, every year on the 15th day of the first month by the lunar calendar, on the Lantern Festival, people made little dragons out of bamboo sticks and coloured paper. They held dragon dances to help later generations remember the Little Golden Dragon's good deeds, and to let him celebrate bumper harvests with the people.

Compiled by Huang Jixian
Translated by Wu Ling

The Bright Pearl

LONG, long ago there was a snow-white Jade Dragon, living in a rock cave on the east bank of the Celestial River. In the great forest across the river lived a beautiful Golden Phoenix.

Leaving their home every morning, the dragon and the phoenix met each other before going their different ways. One flew in the sky, while the other swam in the Celestial River. One day both came to a fairy island. There they found a shining pebble and were fascinated by its beauty.

"Look, how beautiful this pebble is!" Golden Phoenix said to Jade Dragon.

"Let's carve it into a pearl," said Jade Dragon.

Golden Phoenix nodded in agreement. Then they started working on it, Jade Dragon using his claws and Golden Phoenix her beak. They carved the pebble day after day, month after month, until they finally made it into a perfect small round ball. In high spirits Golden Phoenix flew to the sacred mountain to gather dew-drops and Jade Dragon carried a lot of clear water from the Celestial River. They sprinkled and washed the ball with dew and water. Gradually the ball turned into a dazzling pearl.

They had become attached to each other and both loved the pearl dearly. Neither wanted to go back to the cave and the forest. So they settled down on the fairy island guarding the pearl.

It was a magic pearl. Wherever it shone, things grew better. Trees became green all the year round, flowers of all seasons bloomed together and the land yielded richer harvest.

One day the Queen Mother of Heaven left her palace and saw the brilliant rays shed by the pearl. Overwhelmed by the sight, she was eager to acquire it. She sent one of her guards to go in the middle of the night to steal the pearl from Jade Dragon and Golden Phoenix while they were fast asleep. When the guard came back with it, the Queen Mother was very pleased. She would not show it to anyone, but immediately hid it in the innermost room of her palace, to reach which one had to pass through nine locked doors.

When Jade Dragon and Golden Phoenix woke up in the morning they found the pearl gone. Frantically, they searched high and low for it. Jade Dragon looked into every nook and cranny at the bottom of the Celestial River, while Golden Phoenix combed every inch of the sacred mountain, but in vain. They continued their unhappy search day and night, hoping to recover their treasured pearl.

On the birthday of the Queen Mother, all the gods and goddesses in Heaven came to her palace to offer their congratulations. She prepared a grand feast, entertaining her guests with nectar and celestial peaches, the fruit of immortality. The gods and goddesses all said to her, "May your fortune be as boundless as the East Sea and your life last long like the South Mountain!" The Queen Mother was excited and, on a sudden impulse, declared, "My immortal friends, I want to show you a precious pearl which cannot be found either in Heaven or on earth."

So she unfastened nine keys from her girdle and unlocked the nine doors one after the other. From the innermost room of her palace she took out the bright pearl, placed it on a golden tray and carried it carefully to the centre of the banqueting hall. The whole hall was instantly lit by the pearl. The guests were fascinated by its radiance and greatly admired it.

In the meantime, Jade Dragon and Golden Phoenix were continuing their fruitless search. Suddenly Golden Phoenix saw its bright light. She called to Jade Dragon, "Look, isn't that the light from our pearl?"

Jade Dragon stuck his head out of the Celestial River and looked. "Of course! No doubt about it! Let's go and get it back."

They flew towards the light, which led them to the palace of the Queen Mother. When they landed there, they found the immortals crowding around the pearl and praising it lavishly. Pushing through the crowd, Jade Dragon and Golden Phoenix shouted together, "This is our pearl!"

The Queen Mother was so enraged by their claim that she snapped, "Nonsense! I'm the mother of the Heavenly Emperor. All treasures belong to me!"

Jade Dragon and Golden Phoenix were infuriated by her remarks. They protested, "Heaven did not give birth to this pearl, nor was it grown on earth. It was carved and polished by us. It took many years' hard work!"

Shamed and angry, the Queen Mother clutched the tray tightly while ordering her palace guards to eject Jade Dragon and Golden Phoenix. But they fought their way back, determined to snatch the pearl from the Queen Mother. The three struggled over the golden tray with all their might. As the tray shook amidst the tussle, the pearl fell off, rolled to the edge of the stairs and then dropped into the air.

Jade Dragon and Golden Phoenix rushed out of the palace, trying to save it from being dashed to pieces. They flew beside the falling pearl, until it slowly landed on earth. When it touched the ground the pearl immediately turned into a clear, green lake. Jade Dragon and Golden Phoenix could not bear to part from it, and so they changed themselves into two mountains, remaining for ever by the side of the lake.

Since then Jade Dragon Mountain and Golden Phoenix Mountain have quietly stood beside the West Lake. Two lines of an old song are still popular in Hangzhou:

> The gleaming pearl of the West Lake fell from Heaven,
> The flying dragon and dancing phoenix alighted on Qiantang.

Compiled by Xu Fei

Short-Tailed Old Li

BLACK Dragon River in Northeast China wasn't always called by that name. The river got its name after Short-Tailed Old Li settled down there. Originally, an evil white dragon lived in the river. It often flooded the area and harmed the people.

Short-Tailed Old Li was from Yexian County, Shandong Province. On the day he was born, it was very cloudy and the wind blew very hard from all directions from morning on. After the wind eased, it began to rain so heavily that one couldn't see another person from a short distance. That was when Short-Tailed Old Li came into the world.

When the newborn baby started to suckle at his mother's breasts, she immediately fainted. Then his father, who was already wearied by family responsibilities, came back from the fields. Now that another child had been added to the family, he felt even more oppressed. Seeing that the newborn baby was such a black, strange creature, he became angry and hit Short-Tailed Old Li with his spade. The spade cut off a part of Old Li's tail. That's how he became short-tailed. He adopted his mother's surname, so his full name became Short-Tailed Old Li. He had been hurt by the spade so badly that he writhed in pain, broke through the roof of the house with a thunderous roar, flew all the way

in a cloud of sparks to the northeast, and set down in Black Dragon River.

Since Short-Tailed Old Li was from Shandong, he took special care of people from that province. Have you ever heard about this? When you sail on Black Dragon River, you ought to ask: "Is anyone on our boat from Shandong?" If the answer is "yes," you will be safe and sound all through the voyage. Some veteran boatmen on the river always cry "Set sail" in Shandong dialect before they start on a voyage.

Every year Short-Tailed Old Li went back to Shandong to pay his respects at his mother's grave. He did it on May 13, for his mother died on that day. It was always fated to rain on that day. There was a saying among the people of eastern Shandong: "Although a drought may go on for three years, May 13 won't be neglected." Even if it started out sunny on that day, people didn't dry their clothes in the open, because Short-Tailed Old Li was coming back to visit his mother's grave. Quite often he brought local specialities from the northeast to the people of his hometown. With the downpour and gale, there was no telling what good things might be blown down....

It was by no means easy for Short-Tailed Old Li to settle down in Black Dragon River in the first place.

A long time ago, there were large pieces of virgin soil along the river. Because the river often flooded, hardly any people lived on the bank, except for an old man who was bringing the virgin soil under cultivation. One day a dark-skinned young man called on the old man and asked to spend the night. The old man let him stay in the house for a night. On the second day, the young man said, "Grandpa, you see I have neither a home nor a place to go. Will you permit me to live in your house?"

"Why not? I have enough food to feed you. If you want to live here, then live here. If you have a yen to work, then work a bit. If you don't, just rest," the old man replied.

From then on, the young man lived in the old man's house. At first he gathered firewood and did some odd jobs for the old man. Later, when the old man went to work on the wasteland the young man made meals for him. As time went by, the two of them got along very well.

One noon, the old man looked tired when he came back from the wasteland. The young man inquired, "How was it? How many acres of land have you opened up?"

"Not much. It's hard work. The tree roots are difficult to pull up!" replied the old man.

"Let's arrange it this way," proposed the young man. "I'm tired of staying home. This afternoon you stay home and make meals. I'll go to work in the fields."

"Fine!" the old man responded.

So the old man stayed home and the young one left for the fields. After lunch, the old man slept till late afternoon. Curious about how the young man was working, he trekked out to the wasteland, and heard the whistling wind from a long distance. Big trees fell down one right after another, tossing dust and stones high in the air. A black dragon was labouring hard, winding his stumpy tail around trees so big that a man could barely put his arms around them, and pulling them up as easily as a man would pick a young sorghum stalk. The trees were piled high on the ground.

The old man feared he would be killed by the flying stones and clumps of earth if he went closer, so he went back home.

In the evening, the young man came back. The two of them sat down to have supper, and then the old man opened his mouth: "How about the work?"

"Not bad," the young man answered. "But I worked a bit too vigorously this afternoon."

"You couldn't be more vigorous today," the old man commented.

"Why, you saw me?" The young man was a bit surprised.

"Certainly. I thought I'd better have a look at you this afternoon, so I went out to the fields. I saw you only from a distance, because I was afraid of being killed by the falling stones and clumps of earth resulting from your labours."

"Grandpa," the young man smiled. "Since you have seen it with your own eyes, I needn't hide it. I think you are very kind. Can we be friends?"

"Of course," the old man said.

"Grandpa, to be honest, I've made up my mind to settle down here," the young man said.

"If you are determined to settle down here, you are welcome to stay at my house," the old man replied.

"It is the river I want to live in, grandpa!"

"Nobody cares whether you live in the river or not."

"But I can't, grandpa," the young man shook his head. "Someone has occupied the river, so I have to fight to live there."

"Then you fight him."

"But I can't beat him," the young man sighed.

"What can we do about it?"

"You must help me."

"How can I help, since I can't swim?"

"You needn't help me in the river. When I fight him, he will go back to have hot food and soup when he is hungry, since he has a home in the river. For me, however, there is only water to drink when I get hungry. How can I beat him like that? So I need you to prepare some steamed buns and stones and pile them up along the bank. After the battle starts, when black foam bubbles up and black hands stretch out, you throw steamed buns into the river. When white foam bubbles up and the white hands of my opponent stretch up out of the river, you drop down stones. This would be a wonderful favour, if you will do it for me."

"Of course I'll do it. You just go ahead."

The young man then told the older one how many buns and stones to prepare, the places to pile them and the distance between the piles. The old man began to pick up stones and make steamed buns, while the young one went out every day to prepare for the battle. Soon all was ready.

Finally the day of battle came, and the young man stepped into the river. The young man was none other than Short-Tailed Old Li. Then the river started to roil and churn, and one wave after another as big as the roof of a house rolled and ebbed, pounding the banks. Soon the combat started. Following the instructions of the young man, the old man watched the waves closely. Soon black foam and black hands were seen in the river, so he dropped in some buns. Then white foam and white hands were seen, so he tossed in stones. Steamed buns for black hands and stones for white hands, over and over. The two dragons fought from early morning till late at night, and finally Short-Tailed Old Li triumphed over the white dragon.

From then on Short-Tailed Old Li settled down in the river, and the water of the river became dark. So it began to be called Black Dragon River.

Short-Tailed Old Li was really an excellent dragon! After the September 18th Incident in 1931, he even acted against the Japanese invaders. At a crucial moment, two regiments of anti-Japanese volunteers on a wooden ship were trying to break out of the enemy's encirclement, and were almost caught by a Japanese battleship. Just then a small boat rowed by a black-bearded old man suddenly appeared. "Don't panic! Follow me!" he shouted as he leapt onto the wood ship. "Set sail!" he cried, waving his hand. Instantly thick fog shrouded the river and nothing could be seen, while the ship with the old man and the volunteers sailed forward like a flying arrow. As a result, the two regiments of soldiers were saved. When it was clear again, the old man was nowhere to be seen. It is said that only two big characters were left on the side of the ship: "Old Li".

Compiled by Liu Yawen
Translated by Wu Jingchao

The Looking-to-Mother Shoal

MANY, many years ago, there was a severe drought on the plain in the northern part of Sichuan. Trees died, crops withered, paddy fields parched and cracked, and ponds dried up. The flaming sun beat down on the villages day after day.

In a village near the bank of a small river lived the Nie family, which had only two members. The mother, in her forties, was called Mom Nie, and her fifteen-year-old son Boy Nie. Their rented land yielded only a few decalitres of grain, and couldn't feed them. So Boy Nie had to go out to gather firewood and cut grass to earn their living. Boy Nie was rather straightforward and tough. An obedient son of his mother, he liked to help others. Because of his virtues, all the girls and boys in the village got along with him very well. Everybody said he was a good boy.

One morning at cockcrow, Boy Nie put a basket on his back and went out to cut grass as usual. As he was walking toward Red Dragon Ridge, he recalled: "I met Changsheng yesterday, who told me there was a spotted horse in Landlord Zhou's courtyard, presented to him by some man. Because it runs very fast, Landlord Zhou likes it very much and has asked the villagers to cut green grass to feed it." While he was thinking, Boy Nie climbed over the ridge without noticing it.

At the foot of the ridge was Dragon-Changing Gully. In springtime, when there was water, there were quite a number of fish and shrimp, and green grass covered the edges of the gully. But now it was nothing but heaps of pebbles. Boy Nie heaved a sigh. Just as he turned to go elsewhere, he suddenly caught sight of a white shadow running out from behind the temple of the village god. Startled, he cried: "Yikes, it's a white rabbit!"

Thinking that rabbits eat green grass, he threw his basket on to his back and gave chase. He ran on and on until the rabbit disappeared suddenly in Sleeping Dragon Valley, where he found a large patch of green grass. Delighted, he took out his sickle and started cutting. Very soon he cut a full basket of the grass.

For two days in succession, Boy Nie went to the valley to cut grass. Strangely, after it was cut the first day the grass grew up just as tall the second day. Boy Nie said to himself, "Why don't I move the grass home and plant it behind our house?" He hurriedly loosened the earth around the grass and uprooted it. Just as he was about to stand up, he saw under the grass roots a pond of water in which floated a shiny pearl. Happily he picked the pearl up, put it into his pocket carefully and went back home with the green grass.

By this time, the sun had sunk below the hills. Mom Nie was preparing maize porridge at home. Seeing her son back, she complained: "Why have you come back so late?" Boy Nie told her what happened and produced the pearl from his pocket. The pearl lit up the entire room and hurt their eyes. Mom Nie hurriedly told her son to hide it in the rice vat. After supper, Boy Nie planted the grass by a bamboo grove behind their

house.

The next morning, the boy got up very early and hurried to the bamboo grove. But to his surprise, the green grass had withered. He hastened into the room to see if the pearl was still there. When he removed the cover of the rice vat, he cried out, "Mom, come and see, quick!" The rice had brimmed over the vat and the pearl still lay there. Only then did they realize that the pearl was a magic treasure.

From then on, the pearl would produce anything they liked: when it was placed on the rice, there would be more rice; when it was placed on top of money, the money would increase. With the money and rice, the Nies didn't have to worry about their food and clothes. Moreover, when their neighbours were short of food, Mom Nie often told her son to bring rice to them. As a poor man himself, he was always willing to lend one or two litres of rice to those who came for help. Soon, the news spread far and wide and reached the ear of the despotic landlord Zhou Hong who lived in the village. He ordered his steward: "Work out a way to get the pearl for me!"

"My Lord, the Nies are poor," the steward suggested. "We can buy it with money."

Boy Nie was a smart boy, and certainly wouldn't take the landlord's bait. So the landlord and his steward concocted a wicked plan. They would say that Boy Nie had stolen the Zhou family's inherited pearl, and the steward would lead four lackeys to the Nie house to take it. If Boy Nie didn't hand it over, they would just tie him up and take him to the county town to put him in jail. But the plan was overheard by Changsheng, the landlord's herdsman, who slipped out to inform Boy

Nie of the plot and suggested that the Nies run away at once. But just as they were about to leave their home, the steward blocked their way and shouted: "Give me our lord's inherited pearl, and you will be let off. Or else you will be killed today!"

Boy Nie was furious. Pointing his finger at the steward, he said, "Relying on the wealth of the Zhous, you bully the poor everywhere. You say I have stolen the pearl. What evidence do you have?"

The steward ignored him and ordered the lackeys to search the house, but they couldn't find the pearl. The steward glared and asked his men to search Boy Nie's body. Quickly Boy Nie put the pearl into his mouth. The lackeys shouted: "Damn it! Boy Nie has swallowed the pearl."

The steward howled: "Beat him!"

Boy Nie was beaten so severely that he lost consciousness. But dozens of his neighbours came to his rescue, and the steward ran away. The neighbours carried the boy into the room and treated his wounds. Mom Nie sat weeping on the bed, tending to her son.

After midnight, Boy Nie woke up and cried, "I'm thirsty! I want some water!" Seeing that her son was able to speak, Mom Nie was very happy. She hastily handed him a bowl of water. But the water was emptied as soon as the bowl touched his lips. He drank one bowl of water after another, but still asked for more. Finally he simply bent down over the water vat and drank all the water in it. Seeing this, his mother shivered with fear.

"Son, you've drunk so much water. What's matter with you?"

"Mom, I am burning like fire! I want more water."

"You have drunk all the water in the vat. There is no more water in the house!"

"I will go to drink by the river!"

As the boy finished speaking, a golden shaft of lightning crossed the sky, brightening the whole room. Thunder sounded. Boy Nie left his bed and rushed out of the room. His mother ran after him. The further she followed him, the more troubled she became. Soon a river like a grey belt appeared before them. Like a mad person, Boy Nie jumped into the river and began to gulp. Lightning and thunder crashed. He had drunk half the river! Pulling her son's foot, Mom Nie said, "Son, what's the matter?"

Boy Nie looked back, but his appearance had changed: two horns grew from his head, blue tentacles covered his mouth, and red shimmering scales encirled his neck.

"Mom, release me! I shall turn into a dragon and take revenge!"

Thunder and lightning came from the sky, a violent wind brought a torrential rain, the river rose suddenly, and the waves rolled and seethed. Their quiet land became the centre of a maelstrom. Then torches flashed on the river bank. It was the cruel landlord Zhou Hong at the head of his lackeys, leading the search for the Nies. They wanted to cut open Boy Nie's belly to get the pearl.

Boy Nie was burning for revenge. His body had changed into that of a red dragon, but his mother was still holding his foot. Hearing a confusion of voices Boy Nie realized it was the landlord and his lackeys. He spoke to his mother: "Mom, release me now. I want revenge!" With an effort he broke away and tumbled into the river, surging up in an immense wave.

"Old woman, where is your son?" asked Zhou Hong, viciously grasping Mom Nie's shoulder.

"Damn you, Zhou Hong, you have driven my son into the river, and you are still not content. Son, your enemy is here!"

Zhou Hong kicked Mom Nie to the ground and ran to the riverbank to look for Boy Nie. Suddenly red lightning flashed and a crack of thunder roared. A huge wave rushed over the riverbank, sweeping away Zhou Hong and his steward and drowning them in the river. Gradually the wind dropped and the rain ceased.

At daybreak Boy Nie raised his head from the river and said to his mother, "Mom, I'll be going now!"

"Son, when will you be back?" asked Mom Nie miserably. In the surging waves, a vague answer was heard:

"We'll be living in different worlds: the world of man and the world of the sea. If I come back home it will be only when stones blossom and horses grow horns on their head."

Mom Nie understood that her son would never return. Sadly she stood on a boulder and cried out, "Son, son!" When he heard his mother, Boy Nie lifted his head to give her one last look, forming a shoal behind him. Mom Nie called twenty-four times, and Boy Nie raised his head to look back at his mother twenty-four times. The places where Boy Nie turned to look at his mother turned into twenty-four shoals. Afterwards people named them "Looking-to-Mother Shoal".

Translated by Wu Jingchao

The Dragon Eye

AT the foot of a huge mountain lived a bachelor named Black Cui. He owned no land, not even a piece as big as your palm, so he made his living by carrying a pole with tools on it to mend pots and bowls for people. One day, he ran into a baby dragon on his way. He put it into a box and fed it every day. Gradually the dragon grew too big to be kept in the box. Black Cui then placed it in his room. But after only a few years, the room couldn't hold it either. So one day he said to the dragon, "You know that I rely only on my carrying pole for food. Now you've grown so huge that I can't afford to feed you. Let me take you to the cave on North Mountain, all right?" The dragon nodded its head.

After about a year, a ginseng plant grew up at the entrance of the cave. Although everyone knew it was a treasure, nobody dared to pick it, because the dragon guarded it. Later the emperor learned about it and decided he must have it. The magistrate of the prefecture asked around, and discovered that it was Black Cui who had raised the dragon. So he told Black Cui to fetch the ginseng, and threatened to have his head chopped off if he couldn't get it.

Black Cui could only pull himself together and head for the cave. He was still quite a distance from the cave when he saw the dragon lying on its stomach at the cave entrance. "Oh, dragon!" he said. "Save my life in return for my care of you, please! Let me dig up the ginseng!" The dragon nodded its head a second time. Black Cui hoed out the ginseng and handed it in to be sent to the emperor.

After a time, the emperor's wife contracted an eye disease. Good doctors everywhere were invited to attend her. But no matter how hard they tried to cure her, her eyes got worse and worse and eventually she went blind. Someone told the emperor, "A dragon's eye can cure eye diseases. One touch of it can cure."

The dragon was so powerful and huge that even an army couldn't defeat it. Then the emperor thought of Black Cui again. An imperial edict was passed down to Black Cui, saying that if he managed to get a dragon's eye, he would be appointed a minister; if not, his whole family would be killed.

Black Cui was both afraid of death and eager to be a minister. But he knew that this task was very different from the last; last time his task was to seek ginseng, but this time he was going to ask for an eye of the dragon. At last, he had to force himself to go to the cave.

At the cave he said, "The emperor has ordered me to get a dragon's eye. Oh, save my life for the sake of my care of you, please. Let me extract one of your eyes." The dragon listened to him and nodded again. It stayed motionless until Black Cui had cut out its left eye with a knife, and then shed a tear because of the pain.

After he gained the dragon's eye, the emperor touched it to his wife's troubled left eye, and immediately it could see again. When it was touched to her right eye, her two eyes were as good as before. The emperor was so overjoyed that he indeed appointed Black Cui a minister.

Black Cui then started to lead an easy life, enjoying both a high position and great wealth. Slowly he changed into a heartless, malicious man who cared only for his own happiness. He didn't give a thought to other people's suffering. Whatever precious things other people had, he wanted to possess them himself.

Seeing that the dragon's eye was a treasure, he said to himself: I shall ask for the dragon's other eye. So he started on his way in a sedan chair and went to the mountain, and said to the dragon, "Dragon, it was I who raised you! Let me have that right eye of yours as well." The dragon nodded for the fourth time. But when Black Cui got near the head of the dragon to cut out the eye, the dragon opened its immense mouth and swallowed him up in one bite.

Compiled by Dong Junlun and Jiang Yuan
Translated by Wu Jingchao

Only Eight Dragons on the Roof

ALL tourists who visit the Imperial Summer Mountain Resort at Chengde marvel at the gold tiles and the gold dragons on top of the roof of the New Palace. Yet some feel regret on seeing only eight dragons, for by imperial order there should have been nine dragons....

Legend has it that in order to welcome a Living Buddha from Tibet, Emperor Qian Long ordered built a Lesser Potala Palace, one exactly like the Potala Palace, at an auspicious place in Lion Gully. More than thirty thousand ounces of gold was used on just the roof. The hall under it looked quite majestic, and the emperor was extremely pleased. But he felt that the roof needed some decoration. He alloted another ten thousand ounces of gold and ordered that nine dragons be fashioned to lie on the roof. The artisans began to make moulds according to the emperor's design, in which the dragons seemed to be sailing on the roof and floating on clouds. One of the nine dragons was bigger than the rest, and they were all different in posture too looking up or down, running or with their heads turned backwards. After the artisans spent great efforts in making the moulds, something odd happened when they poured molten copper in. All the moulds produced were copper ingots instead of dragons. With more than three hundred artisans working on the project, not one dragon was made although a year elapsed. As the Living Buddha was arriving at any moment, the emperor was enraged about the delay and threatened to kill all the artisans if they could not produce the dragons in a month. The artisans were worried stiff and could only wait for death. One day, the soldiers brought in an old goldsmith who looked at the furnace and said, "When so much gold is to be used for gilding, the furnace must have the offering of boy and girl twins." But no one except the old goldsmith himself had four-year-old boy and girl twins. To save everybody's life, the old goldsmith hardened his heart and decided to make the sacrifice. Knowing that the twins were the apple of his eye, as they had been born when the old man was already fifty, all the artisans knelt down to stop him, preferring to die themselves.

With tears in his eyes, the old goldsmith said, "Let's try once more. If we succeed, we need not give any offerings."

Taken in, the artisans started to melt the copper. When that was done, the goldsmith excused himself and soon returned with a big bundle. When no one was looking he threw it into the furnace. The fire turned bright red, to the surprise of everyone, and the old man said, "It's a good firing. Let's open the furnace."

Nine dragons were successfully turned out of the moulds, and when gilded with gold they were a gorgeous sight.

The emperor was delighted, and gave a banquet in the New Palace to celebrate. But behind the hall the old goldsmith knelt, weeping and burning incense to

his dead twins. His tears collected into a stream. The emperor was startled when rain fell on his head as he was toasting the nine dragons he had designed. The sky was blue and the sun blazed. Where did the rain come from? Suddenly a eunuch cried out, "The dragons have come to life!" As the old goldsmith wept, all nine dragons writhed in agony and also shed tears. Petrified, the emperor heard the sound of crying from behind the hall. He sent men to investigate and they found the goldsmith. The emperor was enraged and ordered the old man beheaded. All of a sudden the biggest dragon on the roof flew down and with one sweep of its tail sent the men tumbling. Then it flew away with the old man on its back. That is why one dragon is missing from the roof of the New Palace.

Compiled by Chu Yanhua and Wang Qi
Translated by Yu Fanqin

Geshan and Dragon Pearl

IN Pizika Village lived two brothers, the elder one called Gelu and the younger Geshan. Gelu was vicious, while his wife was tricky and wicked and played first fiddle in the household. Geshan, on the other hand, was a good honest boy.

Their parents had died when Geshan was twelve, and he had to live with his brother, who never spared his fists or his feet on Geshan. The poor boy lived a wretched life.

A few years later, when Geshan was seventeen, Gelu and his wife, in order to seize all the property left by the parents, plotted to take Geshan's life. It so happened that the court was drafting soldiers. So the heartless Gelu and his wife secretly sold Geshan to a rich man to take the place of his own son, who had been drafted. Geshan would be taken away that evening.

Mother Wang was a kind old woman who liked Geshan for his honesty and industriousness. She took pity on him, and told Geshan what was going to befall him.

Startled, he almost broke into tears. "What shall I do? A clever fellow will extricate himself from a disadvantageous position. I had better flee." So saying, he stuck his sword at his waist and, without going home, ran away.

The moon rose and stars studded the sky. Geshan followed the direction of the Big Dipper. He walked alone, forgetting hunger and fatigue. Where should he go? Tears streamed down his face.

When the sun rose the next morning, Geshan followed the direction of the rising sun, crossing mountains and wading rivers. He was in no mood to appreciate the scenery and birdsong as he hurried along. All of a sudden a gust of cold wind touched his face. Startled, he looked up to see a beautiful lark flying towards him with a poisonous snake in hot pursuit behind her, its long tongue licking out. The lark would be caught any minute. Geshan pulled out his sword and hopped over. The lark darted up and alighted on Geshan's shoulder, while he slashed down at the coiling snake, killing it.

Geshan turned his head. There was no lark, but a beautiful maiden stood there. Surprised, he said nothing and started to go on his way. The girl quickly accosted him.

"Wait, brother. I want a word with you."

"Why, I don't know you at all."

"I'm Longzhu (Dragon Pearl), the third daughter of the Dragon King. I had been out searching for glossy ganoderma and was on my way home when the snake crossed my path. You saved my life. Not knowing a way to show my gratitude, I would like to be your wife. I wonder what you...?" Before she could finish, the girl bowed her head in embarrassment.

Geshan blushed and was secretly pleased, but then he became uneasy when he thought of his wretched life. He told Longzhu, "I'm homeless. I am like a mud Buddha crossing a river: I can't even protect myself.

How can I keep you?"

"You don't have to worry about anything if you'll just take me," Longzhu reassured him.

Geshan consented to marry her. So the two of them kowtowed to Heaven and Earth in the temple and became man and wife.

Three days later, Geshan and Longzhu arrived at the beautiful dragon palace, where Longzhu told of her adventure and her marriage. The Dragon King was delighted with the brave Geshan, who was both upright and clever.

After a few days in the dragon palace, though eating good seafood and living in luxury, Geshan realized he did not like an idle life doing nothing except eating and playing. And he missed his hometown and his life in the world of men. He wanted to go back to the land. So he told Longzhu, "The dragon palace may be good, but life is dull here and I feel lonely. Let's return to the world of men."

Longzhu consented readily, as she felt the same way.

The day before their departure, the Dragon King asked Geshan, "What jewels would you care to have?"

"None. But my hometown has a shortage of water for growing crops. The people do not have enough grain. I would like to have water."

The Dragon King gave Longzhu a magic bottle, and husband and wife returned happily to the world of men.

The following day, Longzhu produced the bottle and Geshan, filling it with water, went up the mountain and poured it down the slope. Instantly the sound of running water was heard, as many streams ran down the mountain into the fields. From then on, the parched land had no lack of water. Making their home with the Tujia nationality, Geshan and his wife led a happy life.

Revised by Tang Shengde
Translated by Yu Fanqin

Two Magic Gourds

A long time ago, eighteen-year-old Wang Xiang lived with his mother in a small mountain village beside the sea. They eked out a meagre existence, the mother sewing and the son cutting firewood for a living.

One hot summer day, when he was cutting wood on the mountain, Wang Xiang sat down under a tree to cool himself. Hearing a bird sing, he looked up to see no birds, but two gourds hanging from two green vines on the tree. Of identical size, the two little gourds were charmingly smooth and glossy. It would be a pity to pick them now, thought Wang Xiang, but other people might take them if I leave them here. He carefully dug out the roots of the vines, took them home and planted them outside his door, watering them every day. The gourds became even more beautiful.

One day, a geomancer from the south came along and offered a hundred taels of silver for the gourds. The young man was surprised. "Why do you offer so much money for these two little gourds?"

"Since you are an honest man, I'll tell you the truth," said the geomancer. "These are magic gourds. When the one in the east is tossed into the sea, the water dries up instantly. The one in the west can knock down any mountain. They can be used as soon as they ripen in August."

Wang Xiang, who had not wanted to part with the gourds, was even more reluctant to sell them when he learned of their magic.

August arrived in no time. The two gourds turned from green to a ripe yellow.

Wang Xiang picked the gourds. He put away the one in the west and, half believing and half doubting, took the other one to the sea to try it out. As soon as he tossed the gourd into the sea the water receded four or five li. The frightened Wang Xiang picked up the gourd and ran for home. After a few steps he turned and saw a swarthy-faced man chasing behind him with a trident in his hand. His legs giving way, Wang Xiang flopped down on the ground and waited for death. Yet the fierce-looking man was extremely kind. He walked up and bowed to Wang Xiang, saying, "I'm a yaksha of the sea and have come on orders from the Dragon King to invite you to the palace. The king wants to have a word with you."

Wang Xiang waved his hands vigorously. "No. No. I won't go. He can talk to me here."

"He would like to see you in his palace. Just now, you nearly knocked the dragon palace down with your gourd. I think he wants to ask a favour of you. If you will comply he will give you anything you want."

The yaksha pulled the young man along. Wang Xiang seemed to be walking in a dream. His rapid heartbeat slowed very gradually.

"In the dragon palace there is a bamboo cylinder which has an endless supply of rice in it," the yaksha told the young man. "Besides, you can also ask for the puppy next to the king so that you can have a companion."

"Right," answered Wang Xiang. "It can keep me company when I'm cutting wood on the mountain every day."

They soon came to the dragon palace, and when the Dragon King saw the honest young man he quickly rose and offered him a seat. "Young man," he said, "your gourd is no plaything. Please don't use it again, and I'll give you anything you care to have."

"I beg your pardon," said Wang Xiang with bowed head. "I didn't realize it truly had such powers. I'll do as you request. But can I have two things from you?"

"What are they?"

"First, I want that bamboo cylinder."

"Sure. Sure. What is the second thing?"

"I want your little dog."

At this the Dragon King hesitated, for the little dog was really his beloved daughter. How could he give her away? Yet he could hardly refuse the young man. He hardened his heart and agreed.

Wang Xiang bowed deeply. Holding the little dog and carrying the bamboo cylinder, he took his leave. When he looked back at the sea, he saw it was full of water again. As it was noon and he missed his mother, he hastened home. The dog barked and barked in his arms until he placed it on the ground, and lo, it turned into a beautiful young maiden. Flabbergasted, Wang Xiang stared hard. "I'm the youngest daughter of the Dragon King, Brother Wang Xiang. If you do not look down on me, let us marry," said the girl.

"That sounds fine. But I'm too poor. You'd have a hard life."

"You don't need to worry about anything if you consent to marry me," said the girl. Wang Xiang nod-

ded shyly.

When he arrived home with the girl, his mother was unconscious for lack of food. The girl took some rice from inside the bamboo, boiled some gruel and fed the old woman. Two bowls of thin gruel soon revived her. On seeing the girl, the mother was so happy that she wanted to arrange for the wedding right away. But their house was too shabby and small. Guessing her thoughts, the girl asked, "Mother, whose vegetable garden is that outside?"

"It's ours."

"All right, then. We'll make do in this little house tonight. Just wait till tomorrow. We'll live in a big house."

The girl rose at midnight, and reciting an incantation she summoned fish, turtles, shrimps and crabs from the sea. They soon built a big house in the garden. In the morning, when Wang Xiang and his mother opened the door, they saw a big tile-roofed house with five rooms and two wings. In the courtyard there were chickens, ducks, geese and dogs. Who built it? "I did," said the girl with a smile. "Let's move into the new house and pull down the old one to plant vegetables."

The mother invited friends and relatives and threw a wedding party that same day.

Before long, the story got to the ears of the county magistrate, who came with a few runners to investigate Wang Xiang's new estate. But what swept him off his feet was Wang Xiang's beautiful wife. So he told the young man, "Wang Xiang, this is a good house. I want to move in too."

"I must get permission from my wife," answered Wang Xiang.

Seeing through his trick, and determined to teach him a lesson, the girl told Wang Xiang, "Let him come. We'll give him the best rooms."

The magistrate moved in that very day. Following the girl with his eyes all day long, he very much wished she could be his own. One day, unable to contain himself any longer, he suggested to the young man, "Give me your wife, Wang Xiang, and I'll give you an official post."

Wang Xiang shook his head in refusal.

"Then you will have to pull down the big willow tree outside the door and plant it upside down. Otherwise you'll have to give up your wife."

Wang Xiang was worried, and went in and told his wife what had happened. His wife said, "You go ahead and have a good sleep. The tree will be planted before dawn."

That night, the girl summoned the fish, turtles, shrimps and crabs again. They dug in the ground, pulled the tree up and planted it upside down. The magistrate came up with another trick. "Well, that is not all. You will have to push down that mountain before us. Otherwise you still have to give up your wife."

Again Wang Xiang went in low spirits to tell his wife. "Haven't you another magic gourd?" his wife reminded him. "It can be useful now."

The following morning, when Wang Xiang made for the mountain, he saw the magistrate and his runners keeping an eye on him at the foot of the mountain in case his wife helped him again. That gave Wang Xiang an idea. He skirted around behind the mountain and placed the gourd at its foot. Crash! The mountain blew up and toppled over, burying the magistrate and his runners.

Wang Xiang and his family lived happily ever after.

Compiled by Liu Renxing and Jiang He
Translated by Yu Fanqin

Princess Anpo

AT the foot of Cockscomb Mountain in Anpo, Xinjin County, is a hot spring called Anpotang which is hot in all seasons and helps cure rheumatism, sores and skin diseases. The water at the mouth of the spring is hot enough to boil eggs.

It is said that long, long ago there wasn't any hot spring here at all, but a big sea which rolled off to the south of Cockscomb Mountain. In a palace in the deep, deep sea lived an old Dragon King who had a beautiful little daughter called Anpo, whom he loved so much that he carried her in his arms all day long.

One day, the old Dragon King heard from someone that if the little princess could be breastfed by a human being, her beauty would increase a hundred-fold. So he came to the world of men on a cluster of cloud, and there he saw a woman breastfeeding a little boy. He kidnapped her and made her feed his daughter.

At first the woman missed her husband and baby so much that she often wept sadly. Gradually, she grew to love Princess Anpo as if she were her own daughter, and the princess became more and more beautiful after drinking her milk. She too looked upon the woman as her kin. The nanny, still missing the human world, often told the princess how charming were the mountains and rivers in the human world, and how the men cultivated the land while the women wove. The little princess, charmed by the stories, wished she could have wings and fly to the human world. One day, when Nanny was again telling her stories, she asked:

"How do you know so much about the human world, nanny? Have you been there?"

"That is where I came from, my child."

"How did you come?"

"Your father kidnapped me," she answered with tears in her eyes.

"Do you have a family there?"

"I live at the foot of Cockscomb Mountain on the north coast of the sea. I have a husband and a son. My son Golden Ox has a mole on his right earlobe. If he is still alive, he would be your age."

The princess was upset. She told her nanny, "When I grow up, I'll go to your home and be your daughter-in-law to show my gratitude to you for bringing me up."

Nanny pulled her into her arms. "I'll be well content to have you as my daughter-in-law," she said.

Time flew by, and the princess turned into a young lady. She decided to go and take a look at Nanny's family.

One day, the old Dragon King took her to a peach banquet hosted by the Queen Mother of the West. The princess found the celestial palace just as quiet and lonely as the dragon palace, and a far cry from the human world described by her nanny. So while the Dragon King was drinking at the banquet, she secretly left the celestial palace and floated down on a cloud to the foot of Cockscomb Mountain on the north coast of the sea. What she saw was not so good: The sun beat

down on a dry, cracked land; the trees, flowers and grass were all withered; people were fleeing from hunger. She wondered how Golden Ox and his father were getting along. She looked around at the foot of the mountain until she came to a little thatched hut outside which hung a torn fishing net. This must be her nanny's home. Standing at the door, she heard moaning inside. On entering, she saw an old man with sores all over his body while beside him sat a young man of about eighteen chasing away the flies for him. The young man was strong, handsome and had a mole on his right earlobe. Secretly pleased, she asked, "What's your name, brother? And who is this old man?"

"My name's Golden Ox and this is my father," replied the young man. "What is your name and where did you come from? Why are you here?"

So this was her nanny's home. But she only told Golden Ox, "My name is Anpo and I came from a long way off to look for my relatives. Not finding them, I don't know what to do."

Finding the young woman not only kind but also attractive, the old man said, "Don't worry if you can't find your relatives. I am afraid you will look down upon us, but if you do not, I hope you'll marry my son."

Remembering what she had said to her nanny when she was a child, and having fallen for Golden Ox too, she flushed and nodded. Golden Ox, though happy, was hesitant. "This natural disaster has made us so poor, dad," he said to his father. "And you are ill. How can we have a wedding?"

Princess Anpo pulled a golden hairpin from her hair and gave it to Golden Ox. "Take it and sell it in the marketplace and get some medicine for Father. Buy some rice and flour with what is left. Then we can have a wedding."

Golden Ox did what he was told, and they were married that evening. The young couple were very much in love. When they went out fishing, they always got a big catch, even when other fishermen came home empty-handed. They sold what they couldn't eat for medicine. But the old man never got well, and more and more people died of hunger. Very worried, Anpo asked her husband one night, "Why is there such a bad drought, Golden Ox?"

Golden Ox sighed. "It is all the doing of the old Dragon King in the sea."

"Why is that?"

"Well, when I was still a child my mother was kidnapped by the Dragon King. When I grew up and learned about what had happened, I pulled down the Dragon King's temple by the sea in a rage. The old Dragon King came, and when he was just about to get me with his claws, my father dashed over and threw himself on me. His back was scratched by the claws, and the Dragon King swore that the place would have no rain for three successive years, threatening to kill all of us. From that time on, sores have covered my father's body and we have had a bad drought." He paused and told his wife, "You mustn't tell anybody about this. Otherwise, the old Dragon King will get angry and make things more difficult for us."

Shamefaced, the princess told him, "To tell you the truth, Golden Ox, I'm Princess Anpo, daughter of the Dragon King. But I never knew he was so wicked."

Golden Ox's eyes bulged and he said in a rage, "The

Dragon King is my enemy. How can I marry his daughter? Besides, when other people learn about this, no one will want you here. You'd better go."

He pulled the princess down from the bed, pushed her outside the door and bolted it. No matter how she pleaded, he wouldn't open it. Weeping, the princess walked towards the sea.

One day in the celestial city equals a whole year on earth. When Princess Anpo returned to the dragon palace, the Dragon King had still not returned from the banquet. Going to her nanny's room, she called her "Mother-in-law" and threw herself weeping into her arms. Nanny was startled.

"What's wrong, princess?" she asked.

The princess tearfully told her what had happened, about her marriage to Golden Ox and how he had thrown her out the door.

Nanny's heart broke on hearing that her hometown was ravaged by disaster and her husband was so ill. Tears pouring down, she told the princess, "I know how to help the people and cure your father-in-law, my child. But it is very risky."

"I'll take any risk to help the people and my father-in-law."

Nanny whispered to her, "On your father's bed there are two bottles of magic water, one warm and the other cold. The cold water can revive all crops and the warm cures all diseases. If you can take these two bottles of water to them, the people and your father-in-law will be saved. But if your father finds out that you've stolen the bottles, he'll condemn you to the hellish inferno and you can never be saved."

The princess plucked a water-repellent pearl from

her hair and gave it to her nanny, asking her to go home for a reunion with her family. The tearful nanny asked her, "What are you going to do, my child?"

"Don't worry, mother-in-law. I'll come soon."

After her nanny left, Princess Anpo stole the two bottles and flew to Cockscomb Mountain. On its peak she opened the bottle of cold water and poured it down. All of a sudden, the south wind rose as thunder rumbled in an overcast sky, and the rain poured down. Already at home, Nanny knew that the princess had succeeded in stealing the magic water. When she told this to Golden Ox, he regretted having blamed her unjustly. He dashed outside and, standing on a big boulder, he called to the sky, "Princess Anpo!"

By this time the parched land had had enough rainfall. On hearing her name called, the princess put the top back on the bottle and instantly the sky cleared up. Looking down from the rainbow she was standing on, she saw the mountain turning green. On the formerly parched land, grass was growing and flowers were blooming. People came out of their homes and began ploughing with oxen. Golden Ox was beckoning to her. She happily descended and walked over to him blissfully.

The old Dragon King trembled with rage when he returned from the peach banquet and learned that his daughter had stolen his bottles and eloped. He came in hot pursuit on a black cloud. When the princess saw him, she told her husband, "I have wanted to be a wife to you all my life. But now my father has come for me. You must go away quickly, otherwise he will send both of us to the hellish inferno."

Holding her tightly, Golden Ox said, "Live or die, I

stay with you."

The Dragon King was mad with fury. He pushed Golden Ox away and with a swish of his tail he cut open Cockscomb Mountain and shoved the princess into the opening, which then closed up again. In his rage, the Dragon King dived into the sea forgetting to retrieve his magic bottles.

Golden Ox's heart broke to see the princess buried in the mountain. He clawed at the mountain for three days and three nights. Although his fingers bled and he was worn out, he did not find the princess.

Buried under the mountain, the princess wanted to come out to see Golden Ox. She opened the lid of the hot water bottle, and boom! Warm water gushed out from the pit Golden Ox had dug with his fingers, filling it and then flowing into a nearby stream.

Golden Ox put his hands into the warm water and instantly his lacerated fingers healed. Knowing it was magic water from Princess Anpo, he went home with tears in his eyes and together with his mother helped his father out and washed his sores. They soon disappeared. When word got around, all the people with sores came to be cured.

Later, to remember this kind-hearted princess, people called the hot springs Anpotang.

Compiled by Song Yiping
Translated by Yu Fanqin

The Story of White Dragon Mountain

A towering mountain outside the west city gate of Zhenjiang is called White Dragon Mountain. Black clouds are said to drift over every night in the small hours, to circle around the mountain and then float slowly to the west before dawn. Why is this? Let me tell you the story.

Long, long ago, White Dragon Mountain, imposing and higher than the clouds and abounding in exotic flowers, grasses, time-honoured pines and cypresses, was called Long Mountain. In it lived a four-legged snake who, after a thousand years of tempering its character, was transformed into a land dragon who in turn was transformed into a beautiful girl dressed in white. People called her White Dragon.

The third day of the third lunar month was the birthday of the Queen Mother of the West. On that occasion she always invited celestial, land and aquatic gods and goddesses to a banquet to feast on the peaches of immortality which grew in her garden, and on the wine made from these peaches. White Dragon, a land goddess, was invited too; and on her way there she ran across a prince who was the third son of the Dragon King of the Eastern Sea. He asked her, "Where are you

bound, miss?"

"The peach banquet."

"Where did you come from?"

"Long Mountain. And you?"

"The Eastern Sea. Come. Let's go together."

All the way, they chatted about all sorts of topics, hitting it off so well that on parting the third prince requested, "Can I call on you tomorrow?"

"Of course. I'll be waiting for you."

Before dawn the next morning, the third prince called on her riding a cluster of clouds, and before they knew it the handsome young man and the beautiful maiden fell in love. After visiting each other a few more times, their love became so intense that they pledged to marry.

But a heavenly rule forbade the celestial, land and aquatic gods and goddesses to intermarry. The aquatic third prince, unable to move about without water, always brought wind and rain on his night excursions to Long Mountain. Finally the Jade Emperor heard of the courtship and sent a god to investigate the situation. He quickly discovered the rebellious rendezvous. So the Jade Emperor summoned the Dragon King of the Eastern Sea and gave him a piece of his mind, telling him to discipline his son.

In a rage the Dragon King shut up his son for three years. But the prince, though in confinement, always had White Dragon on his mind. He gazed at Long Mountain from his crystal palace, thinking of White Dragon, while she, standing on top of Long Mountain and looking towards the Eastern Sea, thought of him. They both grew thin pining for each other.

Since confinement didn't work, the Dragon King

picked out many aquatic goddesses of outstanding beauty to keep company with the third prince, but he had eyes for none of them, and only pleaded the more for permission to see White Dragon.

"This will not be a marriage of equal status, and it violates the rule of heaven," said the Dragon King. "The Jade Emperor will punish not only you but our whole family. If you want to see her, you can go in the night on clouds, but you must not bring wind and rain."

As it was impossible for aquatic dragons to travel without wind and rain, the prince's father was in effect still forbidding him to see his love. He wasted away pining for her.

One day, as the third prince let out a deep long sigh gazing at Long Mountain, a pheasant skipped over and told him, "Don't lose heart, third prince. Take me with you when you go to see White Dragon. I'll crow to remind you of the time to come home. Your father will not know of your excursions."

The prince's spirits instantly improved and, stroking the pheasant, he said, "You're a treasure, pheasant. My father doesn't understand me. But you are a good friend."

Gazing at the distant Long Mountain, the prince let out another deep sigh. How could he go there if his father forbade him to take wind and rain along?

A horse, neighing, galloped over and told him, "Don't lose heart, third prince. Your father can't stop you. You won't need wind and rain if you ride on my back."

Delighted, the prince stroked the white horse, saying, "You're a treasure. My father doesn't understand me.

But you're my good friend."

In the small hours of the following morning, on horseback with a chicken coop in his hand, he made straight for Long Mountain. Instantly, black clouds drifted over, floating around the mountain. The third prince tethered the horse to a pine tree and put his coop on top of a nearby hillock.

Seeing each other for the first time in three years, the lovers' meeting was tearful, and they had endless things to tell each other. Before daybreak, when the pheasant crowed, the third prince snatched up his coop and returned to his palace on horseback.

The two young lovers saw each other every night, and before long, the Dragon King sensed something amiss, wondering how his son had gotten well and why he no longer pined for White Dragon. He kept his eyes open, and discovered that the pheasant and the horse were helping the prince on his romantic visits.

After midnight that day, when the prince started on his trip the Dragon King followed him stealthily. He got so worked up upon seeing him with White Dragon that he hit out with his arm, sending the pheasant in the coop crashing into a hillock, which was ever after called the Pheasant Coop. Then he drew his sword and slashed off the head of the horse, leaving a headless saddled horse. So the spot where the horse stood was called Saddle Hill while Long Mountain became White Dragon Mountain. People used to recite:

To the east of White Dragon Mountain is Pheasant Coop Hillock.

To the east of Pheasant Coop is Saddle Hill.

It is said that the black clouds floating around White

Dragon Mountain are really the loyal horse taking the third prince to see his love. And if you listen carefully you can still hear the crowing of the pheasant in the heart of the hillock.

Compiled by Kang Xinmin
Translated by Yu Fanqin

The Gorge Opened by Mistake

LONG, long ago, a little green snake happened to come to Wushan Mountain in Sichuan, where he found and entered a secluded cave. Stalactites shaped like animals and birds hung down from the ceiling, and from the ground grew beautiful stalagmites as well. Clear spring water dripped down a big stalactite in the centre of the cave into a big square pool, making a beautiful sound just like a zither being plucked.

A bat which lived in the cave told the marvelling little snake, "This is Dragon Water Pool. Legend has it that a thousand years ago, a little snake came here every day to drink. Later he became a dragon and went out to the sea."

"I want to be a dragon too. Can I stay here and temper myself?" asked the little snake.

All the bats agreed.

So the little green snake settled down in the cave and drank from Dragon Water Pool every day, tempering himself in the pool until, three hundred years later, he became a serpent as thick as a bucket. After another three hundred years, when his body was covered with golden scales, he became confident of achieving his aim. Another three hundred years gave him white jade-like horns on his head. Almost a dragon now, he was very pleased, and the bats congratulated him. They were proud to have him as a friend.

A small bat moved up shyly to admire his glittering scales and touch his majestic horns. "A dragon can deploy clouds and water. Can you do that?" he asked.

"Of course I can now that I'm a little dragon." He nodded complacently. "Look at me."

As soon as he opened his mouth he emitted a tall column of water which bored several holes in the cave and killed several bats. He laughed contentedly and gloated, "My. Aren't you useless! I've just barely lifted a finger."

The surviving bats cried and scolded him. They were too indignant to want this presumptuous little dragon to be their friend any more.

The little dragon didn't have claws and a tail to go to the sea yet. Patiently he tempered himself for another three hundred years until he had sharp claws and a beautiful tail.

Midday of the Dragon Boat Festival, which falls on the fifth day of the fifth lunar month, was the time when the dragons went to sea. The little dragon waited patiently, and when that day came he hopped joyfully out of the cave. Immediately he breathed out clouds and rain and proceeded along a little river. When a boulder hindered him, he thought he would try his might. Crash! He dashed against the boulder, breaking it into smithereens to his great satisfaction. Tiny fish, shrimps and crabs came to congratulate him on his power. Yet he turned his nose up at these little things who were no bigger than one of his claws.

The little dragon knocked about in the twisting and forking river, not knowing which way led to the sea.

A carp just returning from the Eastern Sea hastened

over to help the anxious little dragon. "Do you want to go to the sea, little dragon? I can tell you which way to go." The little dragon thought it ridiculous for a dragon to get help from a fish. "Mind your own business," he refused flatly. "I can find my way." Having courted a rebuff, the fish swam away sullenly.

The little dragon, proceeding blindly for some distance, became extremely irritated. An old turtle came along, and from the vexation on the dragon's face knew that he was lost, and so hurried over to help. "Let me lead the way for you, little dragon. I've lived for thousands of years in the river. I know the river inside out."

Then the little dragon really blew his top. He snapped at the fool of a turtle who looked so odd, "Go away, ugly devil. Get lost." With a swish of his tail he sent the old turtle into the sky. The turtle dropped to the ground half dead, saved only by his hard shell.

For three days, the little dragon swam in the forked river without finding the outlet to the sea.

A shepherd was cutting grass on the road beside the river. Men are the cleverest beings, thought the little dragon. He must know the outlet to the sea. I'd better ask him. So he transformed himself into a handsome young man and swaggered over. "Where's the outlet to the sea?" he demanded.

"Go that way...."

The young shepherd pointed east with his sickle, but before he could finish his explanation, the young man transformed himself back into a dragon and dived into the river, frightening the shepherd so that he took to his heels.

The conceited little dragon, finding the shepherd was

a young boy after all and reluctant to learn from him, headed in the direction of the curved sickle's point, which was north, instead of the eastern direction meant by the shepherd boy. He turned a bend and came up against the towering southern slope of Wuxia Gorge, which rose up from the water before him, blocking his advance.

No mountain should block my way, I'm so powerful, thought he. So he raised his head and swept his tail, bringing up a flood to brazen a way through to the sea.

Trees and stones were washed down, but the granite stood unyielding. The furious little dragon let out an earthshaking roar and jabbed his horns at the mountain. Thunder shook the gorges as raging storms and flood water overflowed the banks, inundating houses and fields. People cried and shrieked. Even the monkeys on Wushan Mountain were hit by the calamity. Crying and cursing, they fled into caves and scurried up trees.

Provoked by the monkeys' curses, the little dragon drew in all the river water and then spewed it out against the rocks, sending the monkeys and temples of the Earth God and the Mountain God up into the air. The Earth God came to appease him, "Listen to me, little dragon. Go east in the direction of the sun and you'll reach the sea." The little dragon paid no heed, although the Earth God tired himself out repeating his exhortation many times. The dragon went on dashing against the mountain slope.

The Mountain God flew to the Twelve Peaks on Wushan Mountain and reported the situation to the Goddess of Wushan, who quickly flew to the spot on a cloud and called down, "Listen to me, little dragon. Go east and stop storming the mountain. You'll regret it if you go on like this."

Still turning a deaf ear, the little dragon went about his exploit even more vehemently. I must save the people, thought the Goddess of Wushan, taking out a water-subduing stone and throwing it at the flood water, which immediately abated. The people were saved.

The little dragon dashed his head against the rock until his horns broke and his scales fell off. He continued with all the strength he had accumulated over the years, and succeeded at last in splitting the mountain with a deafening sound, leaving a gap thirty li wide. Later people called this the Gorge Opened by Mistake.

The hysterical little dragon swam to the Yangtze River, where a thunderbolt sounded and three white dragons leapt from the river to swoop down on him. He mistook this for a welcome from his fellow dragons. But the white dragons roared with one voice, "We've come to arrest you for your misdeeds on orders of the old Dragon King." Of course the little dragon would not succumb, and the four dragons turned and rolled about in battle.

The Goddess of Wushan quickly pulled an earring from her ear and threw it into the air. Turning into a golden ring, it dropped like lightning on the little dragon's back, hitting it heavily. The white dragons at once rushed up and caught him.

The Mountain God put a chain around the neck of the little dragon, pulled him onto level ground and fastened him to a pillar.

"Why didn't you go east to the sea instead of knocking about at Wushan Mountain?" asked the goddess.

"The shepherd boy told me to go this way," argued the little dragon.

The Earth God summoned the shepherd boy, who said, "I pointed to the east with my sickle. But instead of listening carefully to my explanation, he dashed off to the north, in the direction of the sickle point. It wasn't my fault at all."

"Following the wrong direction was no crime," retorted the little dragon.

The Goddess of Wushan told the Mountain God to take the little dragon up to the highest peak to show him the harm he had done to the people by storming the mountain with no reason at all. He had to bow his head in shame at sight of the flooded villages and fields.

The bats, the turtle and the monkeys all came to accuse him too. The collective resentment at the little dragon was so great that the Goddess decided to have him executed.

Later, people called the pillar the Subdued Dragon Pillar and the level ground the Dragon's Execution Platform. We can still see these relics beside the Gorge Opened by Mistake.

Compiled by Yan Qinyu
Translated by Yu Fanqin

Baotu Spring

LONG, long ago, in Jinan City, there was a young man called Bao Quan who made a living by selling firewood. He worked all day long, the axe never leaving his hand, yet still he found it hard to support his aging parents. One year, both his parents fell ill. Living from hand to mouth, he had no money to send for a doctor and get medicine. He pleaded with his relatives and friends and borrowed some money. But when the doctor saw the small sum, he refused to see Bao's parents on the pretext of being busy. He turned his back on Bao Quan when the young man pleaded for help. When his parents died one after the other without seeing a doctor, Bao was very sad. He felt so incapable as a grown son that he wanted to die himself. But there were many men as helpless as he. Who would save their parents when they fell ill?

Bao Quan suddenly remembered a monk on the Southern Mountain who had much medical knowledge. He decided to go and learn from him so that he could cure the poor people. From then on, whenever Bao went up the mountain for firewood, he would go to the temple and ask the monk to teach him. Touched by his sincerity, and by the fact that he helped the temple by cutting firewood and carrying water on each visit, the monk accepted him as an apprentice and taught him everything he knew.

Bao Quan studied hard, and within a year was able to write prescriptions. Every time he went up the mountain for firewood, he would gather medicinal herbs too, and then treat the poor people. His medicine was extremely effective. He cured many poor people but refused to accept anything from them, still making his living by selling firewood. As time went by, people far and near learned about the kind-hearted doctor Bao Quan in Jinan City.

At that time there was no spring water in Jinan. People saved summer rainwater in a big pit for winter. But the water was polluted with the dead bodies of cats, dogs and what-not. How could people not get ill by drinking it? And in times of drought, they didn't even have dirty water. For a bowl of well water, rich men demanded a bowl of grain in exchange. Who could afford that?

One year, not a drop of rain had fallen in Jinan. The ground was cracked and all the crops withered. The people were emaciated with hunger. And then a ravaging plague took people's lives in two hours.

Bao Quan ran his legs off, hurrying from this family to that, but people could not even afford to buy the water to boil the medicine he prescribed. Every morning he got up early and walked thirty li to the Big Clear River to get water for those who couldn't afford to buy it.

One day, Bao Quan was panting under a load of water when he heard moaning. Looking around, he saw a lean old man with a white beard lying beside the road, his mouth foaming and seemingly at his last breath. Bao Quan quickly put down his load and took from his pocket some medicine, which he fed the old man with water. Within the time it took to smoke a pipe, he heard a gurgle from the throat of the old man, who gradually opened his eyes. Bao Quan helped him to sit up slowly. The old man looked him up and down and then asked, "Did you give me medicine?"

"Yes. Are you better, uncle?"

"Why did you treat me, young man?" asked the old man.

"My conscience. I wanted to do something for a dying man."

"It's no favour to me, but bad luck." The old man sighed.

"Why, grandpa. How can that be?"

"All suffering is over if I close my eyes. Everyone in my family has died of illness and hunger. By saving me, you'll make me drag out my existence as a miserable, lonely old man."

Bao Quan thought for a moment and told him, "My parents died for lack of money to send for a doctor. I'm alone in the big wide world too, grandpa. I'll support you all your life if you will adopt me."

The old man looked up and measured the honest young man carefully. His face slowly broke into a smile. He nodded to show his consent, and the young man helped him up and took him home.

The old man was concerned for Bao Quan, who was kept busy all day long treating the poor, so busy that he sometimes skipped meals. "It's no easy job curing all the poor, my son. I know of a way, but it's difficult to achieve."

"I'll do anything to cure the people, godfather. Please tell me what it is."

"Water from the Black Dragon Pool on Mount Tai cures plague. One drop of it in a nostril cures all diseases. If you can carry two buckets full back, the people will be saved. But the mountain is far and high, and there are wolves, tigers and leopards."

Bao Quan smiled with joy. "That is nothing to me. I have cut firewood on the mountains day in and day out. I'll start tomorrow morning at cockcrow. You stay home and tell my patients I've gone to get medicine."

At cockcrow, when the sky was still dark, Bao Quan made ready to leave when his godfather gave him a walking stick. "Take this with you. It will save energy when you are climbing the mountain." Bao Quan accepted it and made straight for Mount Tai.

In his eagerness to bring back water, Bao Quan started before daybreak and walked until way after dark each day, and arrived at the foot of Mount Tai in three days. With the help of his godfather's walking stick he climbed effortlessly and reached Black Dragon Pool halfway up the mountain. The pool was deep though small, and the water in it was azure blue. He filled his hands and took a sip. It was cool and sweet. If Jinan could have water like this, thirst, illness and drought would not threaten people any more. He wanted very much to go to the mountain top to drink in the enchanting scenery, but at thought of the poor sick people, he lowered a bucket into the pool hooked on his walking stick, which had a dragon head carved on the end. But the stick bored into the water with such force that it pulled Bao Quan into the water. He had been holding on with all his might, afraid of losing the stick. I will die, thought he with closed eyes, not knowing how to swim. He drifted along as water gurgled around him, and soon felt he was standing on solid ground. Then he opened his eyes to find a glazed palace with glittering walls, windows and door. He was marvelling at this when a spirited old man emerged from the door, complaining, "What man has the nerve to come to my dragon palace?"

The words "dragon palace" frightened Bao Quan, who quickly bowed to the Dragon King, saying, "I came to get water from Black Dragon Pool to cure the poor of their illness, and carelessly fell down here. Don't be angry with me, please."

The Dragon King smiled. "Take it easy. My nephew has told me about you. Stay a few days now that you are here. I'll take you home."

Bao Quan was reassured, but wondered how the king's nephew knew about him. It suddenly came to him that the walking stick must have been a small dragon, since it pulled him down into the water with such force. Too shy to ask confirmation of the Dragon King, he pleaded his own case: "Let me go home now, please. One day's delay means the death of many people."

"I'll take you with me when I go to the Eastern Sea on the second day of the second lunar month. That's the time I go there every year and that's three days from now. Just take it easy for a few days."

Bao Quan had to comply, yet the jewels, jade, silk and good food in the dragon palace excited no interest in him at all. Three days later, the Dragon King summoned him to the sitting room and told him, "I'll disclose to you that the old man you saved is my brother, who sent his son to ask me to give you something to show his gratitude. What would you like?" Bao

Quan became brave, since his godfather was no ordinary person. Remembering the jade teapot from which the Dragon King had poured sweet, cool water for him, from the spout of which water had flowed freely, he said, "I'd like to have that teapot of white jade."

Fingering his beard, the Dragon King smiled. "I have countless priceless jewels. Why did you choose this teapot?" he asked.

"Jewels may be priceless, but they are useless in curing diseases, while countless people can be cured with water from this teapot."

The Dragon King hesitated. "This teapot is a treasure too, a family heirloom. It has an endless supply of water. Since you saved my brother, I'll give it to you."

Overjoyed, Bao Quan put it carefully in his pocket.

"How do we go?" he asked.

"Hang on to my clothes and don't open your eyes whatever happens. You can only open them when you feel the ground under your feet."

Bao Quan did what he was told, and at the sound of a thunderbolt, wind and rain, he felt himself rising up. After a long time he felt solid ground under his feet. Slowly he opened his eyes and saw he was standing in his own courtyard. Have I been dreaming? he wondered. But he had a jade teapot in his pocket. He rushed happily into the house, calling his godfather, but the room was empty. He saw a poem on his wall, which must have been written by the old man:

The Dragon King gives a jade teapot
To the kindest man in the big wide world.
With water in the teapot,
We'll have no more fear of disease and drought.

Neighbours coming to see him filled his room. Bao Quan realized that his godfather had returned to the Eastern Sea when someone told him, "The day after you left a crane flew down from the sky and alighted on the stone bridge. Then it flew to the east with your godfather on its back."

Bao Quan poured a cup of water for everybody from the jade teapot. The ill were instantly cured and the healthy felt even healthier. Word soon spread through the whole city, and endless numbers of people came for treatment from the miracle-working doctor. When the magistrate got wind of it, he thought: If I could get hold of the magic teapot and give it to the emperor, I would get promotion even to the first rank, and have gold and silver, wives and concubines, anything I care to have. He sent for a runner and told him, "Take ten taels of silver and buy the teapot from Bao Quan. If he won't part with it, borrow it for me."

When the runner came, Bao Quan realized that he couldn't keep the teapot. But the poor would suffer and die from the ravaging drought and plague with the teapot gone. Seeing his reluctance, the runner said, "My lord told me to borrow it even if you refused to part with it." Knowing that the magistrate would never return it, he suddenly came up with an idea.

"This is only an ordinary teapot, sir. But it is an heirloom of my family. I really cannot sell it. I'll lend it to your lord, but please return it soon." He handed over an ordinary teapot which he had been using. The runner grumbled, "My lord must be mad. With ten taels of silver he could get a hundred such teapots!" Then he left with it.

Bao Quan thought to himself, though he had sent

this runner away, the magistrate might send other runners when he discovered the teapot was a fraud. He filled a jar with curing water from the jade teapot, and then dug a deep pit in the courtyard and buried it.

Not getting any water from the teapot brought back by the runner, the magistrate was mad with fury. "You are a fool, accepting this as the magic teapot. Go and bring that cunning man to me."

Bao Quan had barely buried the pot when runners came and took him away.

The magistrate said cunningly, "My jade teapot has been stolen. Where did you hide it? Out with the truth, quickly."

"My jade teapot handed down by my ancestors was stolen too," retorted Bao Quan. "How can I get it back?"

"Thrash him," roared the furious magistrate. But however badly he was beaten, Bao Quan insisted that his pot had been stolen. At his wit's end, the magistrate ordered the runners to find the pot by all means, even if they had to dig three feet deep in the ground.

The runners ransacked Bao Quan's home. Then they forced the villagers to dig up the ground in the courtyard until dark. A big pit was dug, and still no sign of the pot. The runners made the villagers light firewood and jumped down into the pit to dig on. Sure enough, they uncovered the jade teapot. Overjoyed, the runners all wrestled for the teapot in order to get the reward. But the pot seemed to have grown roots. The runners pulled at the spout, the handle, and dug around it at the bottom until a loud sound like muffled thunder rumbled and a huge column of water spurted out from the ground, hurling the runners up into the air and then dropping them into the pit to drown. The powerful column spread water all over the city, which formed many springs. After that, Jinan was known as the City of Springs.

People were cured by drinking the spring water, and crops grew in abundance. They had no more fear of drought from then on.

The furious magistrate, unable to get the jade teapot though he had lost many runners, had Bao Quan killed.

In remembrance of Bao Quan and his godfather, the people named the spring in Bao Quan's courtyard Bao (treasure) Spring, and the bridge from which his godfather had left with the crane Crane Bridge. And as water spurted with a "tu" sound from the spring, the people finally called the spring Baotu.

Compiled by Han Mei
Translated by Yu Fanqin

The Legend of Green Dragon Pond

THE largest park in Tianjin is called Water Park. Its original name was Green Dragon Pond. Why was it called that? Well, let me tell you a story.

Tianjin is at the mouths of nine rivers in which, it is said, lived nine dragons. So that the nine dragons would become his loyal followers, the Dragon King married his nine daughters to them.

On the Dragon King's birthday, all his daughters and sons-in-law came to congratulate him. But by noon, the Dragon King's youngest and dearest daughter Princess Flower and her husband Green Dragon had not turned up. The Dragon King waited and waited until it was afternoon, but there was still no sign of them. The Dragon King became so worried that he ordered Prime Minister Turtle to command the shrimp soldiers and crab generals to look for them along the way.

As a matter of fact, Princess Flower and Green Dragon had left the Daqing River early that morning, mounting the clouds and riding the mist to rush to the sea. But when they reached Liqi Village outside the southern gate of Tianjin, they caught sight of a sad scene. Drought had hit the area so severely that the tree leaves had become yellow, the crops dry, the flowers withered, and people had no water to drink. This made Green Dragon impatient, and he raised his head, about to chant incantations to bring on a torrential rain. The princess quickly stopped him by saying, "Don't be impatient, husband. A torrential rain at a time like this would be too much for the withered flowers, plants, trees, crops, animals and human beings. We'd better spread a gentle rain."

"You're right, princess," said Green Dragon. "I was too impetuous."

This said, Princess Flower began to plough clouds in the sky while Green Dragon spread rain over the land. Talking and laughing, the young couple busily scattered a fine rain on the dry fields.

By afternoon, in the good rain, trees and crops turned green and flowers bloomed, while people of every age happily carried clear water home from the river in big buckets and small jars.

The Prime Minister Turtle and the shrimp soldiers and crab generals came up to greet Green Dragon and Princess Flower. "*Aiya!*" they cried suddenly, "you've courted disaster, Your Excellencies!"

"What trouble have we fallen into?" Green Dragon and Princess Flower asked in unison.

"You don't know yet," Prime Minister Turtle said. "The cunning people in Weinan are very abominable. They refused to build temples for our king. Neither did they like to carve an image of our king to worship. What's more, this spring our king travelled to this place, and was given the cold shoulder. Our king lost his temper and decided not to give this area a drop of rain for ten years, so as to let those hateful people die of famine." He stopped to cast a look at Princess Flower

and Green Dragon, who were still busy ploughing clouds and sowing rain, and then continued, "This region does not come within your jurisdiction, so why are you doing that? If the king blames you, what can you two do?"

"Bringing rain to the human world is our duty, our mission," Green Dragon said angrily when he heard Prime Minister Turtle's words. "How can we use our power just according to how we are treated?"

"If the king complains, my husband and I will take the responsibility," Princess Flower told Prime Minister Turtle.

"The king is waiting for you at his palace," Prime Minister Turtle told them. "He sent me here especially to escort you."

"You go back to report first," the princess said. "My husband and I will continue to sow another three fingers of rain. We'll go to congratulate our father on his birthday immediately after the signs of drought disappear."

After Green Dragon and Princess Flower sowed another three fingers of rain, no more signs of drought could be seen. But as they raised their heads, they saw the angry Dragon King suddenly appear in the sky to the north. They hastily knelt down on the clouds to greet him.

"You little Green Dragon!" the Dragon King shouted. "You have dared to disobey my orders, and to spread rain presumptuously. Why have you done this?"

"But I didn't know your orders," Green Dragon retorted.

"You even dare to defy me!" The Dragon King flew into a rage. "Why did you continue to sow rain even after Prime Minister Turtle told you my orders?"

"Sowing rain is my bounden duty. How could I fail to do it?" replied Green Dragon.

"You have your own area. This region is under my jurisdiction. Why should you poke your nose into my affairs?" The Dragon King bared his fangs and brandished his claws.

"What do you mean, poking my nose into your affairs?" Green Dragon gave tit for tat. "Is it wrong to save these people from dying?"

The Dragon King was furious. Raising his sword, he shouted to the shrimp soldiers and crab generals: "Tie him up and have him beheaded."

"It was I who ploughed the clouds," Princess Flower said, rushing up to her father. "It was also I who asked Green Dragon to sow the rain. Please release my husband and kill me instead."

The Dragon King pushed his daughter aside, brandished his sword and ordered: "Take him to the sky above Liqi Village and behead him. I'll see who will dare to sow rain again!"

After three cracks Green Dragon's head was cut off, but not a drop of blood came out. What gushed out was a stream of clear water, which ran toward the human world below and formed a large pond near Liqi Village. Ever since then people have called this pond "Green Dragon Pond".

Compiled by Sun Shufang
Translated by Xiong Zhenru

Dragon Mother's Temple

THE fatuous Jade Emperor, paying no attention to public affairs, hid himself deep in his palace to seek pleasure all day long. Whether the people lived or died, he did not care. When the Milky Way was breached, he did not send people to repair it, nor did he issue orders to send rain when drought hit the land south of the Yangtze River. Soon the crops withered, rivers dried up, the fields were littered with corpses, and everywhere was a scene of desolation. Finding it intolerable to see people plunged into an abyss of misery like that, the kind-hearted Green Dragon broke the imperial rules by stealthily mending the Milky Way during the day and scattering rain at night. Soon the land recovered and the people rejoiced. But the imperious Jade Emperor could not tolerate any disobedience, and had Green Dragon beheaded.

The pitiful Green Dragon was cut into several parts, and his blood-stained head and body rolled downward to land on a peak of Whitewater Mountain in the Kuocang Range. When it landed, there came a flash of red light and three coloured dragon eggs rolled out from the wounds. The three eggs rolled and rolled until they reached the world of men.

The three eggs kept rolling and passed through forests and grasslands. One day they rolled to a Chinese francolin and pleaded with the bird to hatch them. But the Chinese francolin, who was so lazy she did not hatch her own eggs and had to ask the magpie to do it for her, shook her head and flapped her wings a few times before flying away.

The eggs continued to roll on. Nobody knows how long and how far they travelled before they plopped into a stream at the foot of Whitewater Mountain. The stream ran through forests and deep mountains with water gurgling along the way. The three eggs drifted along the stream and reached a willow tree, where a young cow was drinking water lavishly. Gladly the eggs jostled each other, intending to enter the cow's mouth to be hatched in its warm belly. But the cow shut its mouth and gritted its teeth when it sipped water, and after it drank its fill, wagged its tail and walked away.

Though rebuffed everywhere, the dragon eggs did not lose heart but kept on drifting along the stream. One day they reached a river port where a girl was washing clothes. Very pleased, they began to circle enticingly in the water.

Finding these eggs interesting, the girl immediately scooped them up and fondled with admiration. After a while she carefully put them on a rock, intending to take them home after she finished washing. But no matter how carefully she set them on the rock, she could not steady them, and as soon as her hands moved away, they began to roll toward the water. She put them in her basket, but the meshes of the basket were too big to hold them. She wanted to put them in her pocket, but feared that she might crush them. In despair, she thought it a good idea to hold them in her mouth until she finished her washing. But as soon as she put them in her mouth, they immediately slipped down into her belly.

In a moment, the girl felt nauseated and giddy, and in a faint she saw a green dragon without its head. It told her how it had sown rain for the people and been killed by the Jade Emperor. It pleaded with her to hatch the eggs into dragons so as to relieve people from drought.

When she recovered consciousness, sure enough, she felt something squirming like a snake in her belly. She felt burning hot.

After that the girl changed every day. Her belly grew bigger and bigger and she couldn't eat any food. All she wanted was water. At the beginning she drank a bottle of water each time, but later she had to drink a big jar. Sometimes she was so thirsty at night she had to go stealthily to the stream to drink up half of it.

The news that an unmarried girl had a big belly quickly spread throughout the village. The girl's father flew into a rage from shame, and often cursed and beat her, trying to get her to name the father. Her mother sighed and wept day and night, anxious to discover her secret. No matter how the girl explained, her parents did not believe her. Time passed, and the girl's belly grew bigger. It seemed she would give birth soon, but her parents still could not find out the man's name. Finally, her father decided to lock her up in a pavilion and strangle the infant the instant it was born.

But strangely enough, three years and six months passed and the girl still did not give birth. This drove everyone to desperation. Her father cursed, her mother fretted, and even the girl herself was extremely worried. That year the Jade Emperor did not send rain, and the drought created a stir in the whole village. All the people said that the girl had become a mischief-maker, who had offended the gods and caused the disaster. The local gentry and sorcerers intimidated the girl's father. They said that unless he strangled his daughter they would destroy his family and burn down his house.

Thrown into confusion by the threat, the girl's father decided to hand her over to the local gentry to let them punish her. His decision so worried the girl's kind-hearted mother that she secretly went to the pavilion and warned her daughter to run away as quickly as possible. Falling on her knees to her mother, the girl said, "Mother, I'll probably have no chance to return after I leave home. For the sake of friendship between mother and daughter, I plead with you to come see me in the future. I'll die content if we can meet again!" Her mother helped her up and dried her tears. But they welled up like spring water and could not be dried.

Just then, the gong sounded in the village and the head of the clan shouted at the top of his lungs. He summoned the villagers to the ancestral hall, where they were going to try the girl. The girl's mother hurriedly took the girl downstairs, fetched a small parcel of rapeseeds from a cupboard, put them into a bamboo pole and handed it to her daughter, saying, "You can use this bamboo pole as a walking stick and walk eastward along the stream. I'll go to see you next year when the rape blooms." She walked her daughter outside and only after the girl vanished in the darkness did she turn back and shut the door in tears. At that moment the gong sounded more urgently, and under the light of torches, a big crowd of gentry, sorcerers and

sorceresses, following the head of the clan, came swarming toward the girl's home.

After leaving home, the girl walked along the stream toward the east day and night, crossing high mountains and deep valleys despite numerous difficulties. Her bamboo walking stick had a marvellous tiny hole at its bottom, through which the rapeseeds were evenly scattered on the way. She underwent all kinds of hardships and difficulties until one day she came to Cockscomb Cliff on Xiandu Mountain. By then she was too exhausted to move any farther. The burning sun overhead and the scalding rocks underfoot made her extremely thirsty. She wanted to drink some water, but every stream had dried up; not a drop of water could she find. She felt faint and dizzy as if the earth were spinning round and round. Suddenly she collapsed at the foot of Cockscomb Cliff.

Cockscomb Cliff was very precipitous and several leagues high, and a stream of spring water coming out of a cave trickled sluggishly along the crevices. Although there was a severe drought, here was a green world with grass growing in the crevices and wild flowers giving off their fragrance.

The girl plunged into a thick growth of grass on the ground at the foot of the cliff, with her face turned downward against the earth. Gradually the damp soil moistened her chapped lips, softened her hardened tongue and refreshed her heart, and she slowly came to.

As she sat up to look around, she found drops of water coming down from the crevices in the cliff. She listened and heard the sound of running water from the top of the cliff. Water was life! Her morale boosted, she climbed up along the stream to look for the source of the water. Although the cliff was so steep that birds found it difficult to fly over and monkeys could not pass over it, the girl climbed it step by step, grasping tree branches and vines, and left her footprints deep on the precipices.

At the top of the cliff she found a natural cave from which the water ran out. Completely forgetting all her fatigue, she rushed to the fountain and drank to her heart's content, and then she settled down in the cave.

Soon it was the next year. After the girl left home, her mother wept day and night and fell ill, unable to forget how her daughter had pleaded with her to go and see her. But she had cried so much that she became blind and deaf. How could she go to find her? She consulted her husband and asked him to go for her. By then the old man had been overcome with regret and wanted his daughter back. But how could he find her in such a big world? His wife suddenly remembered the bamboo walking stick and the rapeseeds.

"Where our daughter walked, there will be a trail of rape flowers," she told her husband. "If you follow the rape flowers, you'll surely find her."

Taking some solid food with him, the old man set off. As he pushed open his courtyard gate, sure enough, he found a column of yellow rape flowers zigzagging into the distance. Following the flowers, he climbed high mountains, passed deep valleys and finally came to Cockscomb Cliff on Xiandu Mountain, where the flowers came to an end and a precipitous cliff barred his way. He discovered some rape flowers and footprints on the steep precipice. Is my daughter up on the cliff? he wondered. Following the footprints, he climbed up the cliff and found more rape flowers waving in the breeze. Thinking that his daughter must be among the flowers, he shouted at the top of his lungs, with mixed feelings of grief and joy: "Daughter!"

"Here, father!" his daughter's voice came out from behind the rape flowers.

"Boom! Boom!" Instantly the sky turned dark and the earth shook. With a flash of red light a little red dragon dashed out from the cave toward the sky, and with a flash of blue light a little blue dragon flew out toward the Eastern Sea....

The girl had been sitting in the cave. On hearing her father's voice, she became greatly excited and opened her mouth to answer. Just as her mouth opened, the two little dragons took the opportunity and flew out of it. Her stomach felt greatly relieved. But just as she opened her mouth to call her father again, a flash of white light came and a third little dragon with silvery white scales dashed out of her. She smiled and her teeth caught a section of the dragon's tail. Turning its head back, the dragon was very reluctant to leave.

"Go ahead, child!" the girl said to the silvery white dragon. "Go to the sea. But don't forget to sow rain for the people every year. And don't forget the mother who's bred you. Come back to see me and your grandmother every year." The silvery white dragon nodded knowingly and flew away.

After he regained consciousness from the shock, the girl's father hurried to the cave and found the girl sitting with her two hands pressed together and her eyes closed. She had died and gone to heaven. Only then did he realize he had wronged her. But it was too late to repent.

The three little dragons were infinitely resourceful

and fought wherever the Jade Emperor forbade the sowing of rain. Their roars were the thunder and lightning, and the Jade Emperor could no longer stop the sowing of rain.

The tailless silvery white dragon came back to see its mother and grandmother every year around the Qingming Festival. Each time it came, it brought with it auspicious clouds and good rain, and after that each year saw favourable weather and a bumper harvest.

To commemorate the girl and to express their gratitude to the silvery white dragon, people called the stream where the girl swallowed the dragon eggs Dragon Stream, and built a temple at the top of Cockscomb Cliff and called it Dragon Mother's Temple. On the night of the 15th of the first lunar month every year, they carefully made all sorts of dragons and paraded them through the streets of the cities and the villages to welcome the dragon to usher in a new year of good harvests.

Compiled by Zao Zhourui and Xiang Quan
Translated by Xiong Zhenru

Tripod Lake and Golden Lotus Flowers

THIS story took place in 2697 BC, during the reign of Huang Di, the traditional ancestor of the Chinese people. It was the year of the very first of the ten Heavenly Stems (used as ordinal numbers and also in combination with the twelve Earthly Branches to designate years, months, days and hours). In order to celebrate a victory over Chiyou (a head of the Jiuli tribes), Huang Di had an eleven-metre-high tripod cast.

On the day of the celebration, tens of thousands of people came from all directions. Even the gods descended from Heaven to congratulate the ruler. The heavenly drums were beaten and the magic bells rang, rainbows hung in the sky, and hundreds of flowers bloomed on the ground. In this bright and colourful world, dragons flew, tigers leapt, cranes danced and orioles sang, deers took glossy ganoderma in their mouths and magic monkeys presented immortality peaches. Fairies danced in the sky, and officials and subjects toasted one another. Both Heaven and Earth were astir with jubilant crowds.

At noon, following a bright flash, colourful clouds floated down. After the clouds dispersed in the vast blue sky, a gold-scaled, glimmering red dragon slowly descended. Finally it put its head on the tripod with its beard hanging down to the ground, while its body still swayed in the sky. Then all the dances and music stopped, and animals and birds, fairies and mortal people all gazed at the dragon.

Huang Di was delighted, for he knew the dragon had come to take him to Heaven. He rose slowly on the golden lotus and mounted the dragon, which then ascended slowly towards the sky....

Seeing this, people knew that their ruler was leaving for Heaven. Who did not want to go to Heaven? They tried to get on the dragon's back. So many people seized the dragon's beard to try to climb up that quite a lot of it was pulled out. The hairs of the beard became Chinese alpine rush, which is called Dragon-beard Rush even today.

As Huang Di gathered many people and took them to Heaven from this place, it was then called Xiandu (Fairy Capital). It is now in Jinyun, Zhejiang Province. In Xiandu there was a mountain, Mount Danfeng, which was several hundred leagues high. On its top was a pit, which was said to appear after the heavy tripod had sunk into the mountain. As time went by, water gathered and people called it Tripod Lake.

In the lake there were some golden lotuses which Huang Di had stepped on to ascend the dragon, and later they grew in the whole lake. The beautiful fragrant flowers attracted people, who all came to pick them. When the Jade Emperor saw this scene, he swept all the lotuses to Heaven in a gust of magic wind.

But unexpectedly two small petals were left which floated slowly in the sky. Finally one petal fell on a hill in Dongyang, and gradually grew bigger, glimmering during the night like a flower in early blossom. People were so surprised that they called it Jinhua (Golden Flower). The hill is today's Jinhua Hill, and the county at the foot of the hill is called Jinhua County. The other petal fell on Xiandu Hill and became a huge rock supporting Wenyu Pavilion, and was called "Green Lotus".

Compiled by Chen Weijun
Translated by Wu Ling

Meidan the Dragon's Daughter

NEAR the city of Xuanping stands Five Dragon Mountain. It abounds with wild flowers, verdant grass, towering bamboos, twisting trails, and trickles and brooks which finally empty into Kettle Lake. Strangely, the crest of the mountain is completely bare, with not a single plant, but instead an enormous stretch of grass known as "horsewhips" which comes to life in spring and summer and dries up in autumn and winter. Stranger still is that the highest peak, called Meidan Peak by folks nearby, which rises into the sky wrapped in pure white. There is a local saying: "When Meidan is dressed in white, it rains during the day; when Meidan has a hood over her head, there will be drought." This is the story behind the saying.

Once upon a time there was a pool called Whitewater Pool. On the day when spring changed to summer an enormous inundation would drown the fields and wash away people and draught animals. But when fall ended it would dry up completely with not a drop of water left. People were forced to travel long distances for water, and prayed to the gods to fill this hateful pool.

A girl named Meidan lived to the east of the pool. Her parents had both been drowned in a flood. She had searched the pool a hundred times but failed to retrieve their bodies. Heartbroken and exhausted, she sat down

by the pool and burst into tears.

Suddenly a wail was heard in the distance. Presently she saw a wolf biting into the hind leg of a young river deer. Meidan let out a loud cry, which scared the wolf away and so saved the deer's life. Meidan then dressed its wound carefully, saying, "Go back home to your father and mother."

To her surprise the river deer, stretching its leg, began to talk. "My saviour, if you ever want anything, just come to the Eastern Sea, where you will find an ancient banyan tree with four branches. Just tap three times on the tree and then call out 'Black Dragon' three times."

In no time it was summer again. All the villagers were packing their things to flee the village when Meidan remembered what the young river deer told her and rushed all the way to the Eastern Sea. Seeing the huge banyan tree, she went over, tapped three times on the trunk, and called out loud to the sea, "Black Dragon, Black Dragon, Black Dragon!"

Her words had not quite died away when there emerged on the crest of the waves a handsome young man. At his gesture the sea cleaved open clear and blue. She felt herself carried away by a gentle breeze until finally she reached the gate of a magnificent palace where the Dragon King and his four sons lined up at the entrance to meet her. Then she was led into the palace by the Black Dragon.

"Dear Meidan, you've saved the life of my youngest son and for your kindness we will repay you. Come, tell us what you want," said the Dragon King.

"I have no parents, no siblings. I came here just to...."

"That's easy." The Dragon King was all smiles. "If

you don't mind, I can take you as my own daughter, so you too will have a family." So saying, the Dragon King took Meidan to be presented to the Dragon Queen and his children. He took a cupful of wine, drank the first mouthful and then shared the rest with his family and Meidan. In this way Meidan was made a daughter of the Dragon King.

Meidan enjoyed her life in the dragon palace so much that she forgot all about what she had come for. It so happened that one day when she was frolicking in the sea with her brothers and sisters she saw a big fish gulping down a human leg. "Where does that human limb come from?" she asked.

"It was washed here by the waves from Whitewater Pool. All the corpses from there are in fragments," answered the Black Dragon.

Meidan, suddenly remembering why she had come to the dragon palace, broke into tears. Try as they might to console her, she was not to be pacified. Finally Black Dragon pulled her hands away from the face, saying, "Elder sister, just tell us what is on your mind and we will do our best to help you."

Wiping the tears from her face, Meidan related how Whitewater Pool went wild every year, claiming thousands of victims and driving many more away from their homes. She begged her brothers and sisters to drain the pool with her and then fill it with stones.

They thought this would be easy and sent to the Dragon King for approval. But he refused point blank. "The water of that pool is preserved for the Queen Mother of the West. At the beginning of every summer the Queen Mother sends gods to empty her Jade Pond into Whitewater Pool, where it is purified and stored up to be transferred again in the fall back to the Jade Pond. So by emptying the pool you would offend Her Majesty."

Argue as they might, the Dragon King was adamant. In the end Meidan went back to her room and wept.

The Black Dragon, seeing Meidan in anguish, went to consult his elder brothers. Together the four brothers came to Meidan's room and said, "We won't have the Queen Mother torturing people. We will set out tomorrow to fill the pool."

So the next morning at daybreak Meidan and her four brothers came to Whitewater Pool. It so happened that the Jade Pond was being emptied that day, and the flood was driving people nearby to flee for their lives. At this sight Meidan shouted out, "Dear people, we've come to fill the pool!"

Seeing Meidan and the four black dragons, people dropped their things to meet them. Presently the four black dragons, displaying their exceptional powers, drank up the pool to the bottom. Then they carried rocks from mountains far away and dumped them into the pool. But the rocks turned instantly into mud at the bottom, refusing to pile up. At this point people went to get bucketfuls of urine and dumped it over the mud, which solidified into rocks at once, thwarting the gods' trick. All went on well enough with the filling of the pool until the Mountain God went to report it to the Jade Emperor. The Queen Mother, boiling with rage, immediately sent some gods to stop it. Seeing the pool filled up when they arrived, the heavenly forces shot thirty-six heavenly arrows at Meidan and her four brothers, who were all fatally wounded. Meidan jumped up to help her brothers, and the five of them turned slowly into a mountain.

Later people had a magnificent temple built in the mountains dedicated to the five dragon children, where they offered sacrifices and prayed to them. They never built temples for the Mountain God, the Jade Emperor and the Queen Mother. Local people were convinced that the dragon children were still alive, for they would suck up the pool to water the meadow at the mountain peak on rainy days and draw it off for people to water their vegetables with in autumn and winter, while letting the grass dry up at the crest of the mountain. Meidan, whose head was high up in the clouds, would have a piece of cloud draped over her shoulders when it was going to rain, and wear a piece of cloud over her head when it cleared up. By and by the mountain peak came to be known as Meidan Peak.

Compiled by Zhong Fapin
Translated by Li Hong

The Dragon King's Daughter and Guanyin

BY the side of Guanyin Bodhisattva are often seen an innocent boy and a maiden. The boy is called Shancai and the maiden Longnu. Longnu was the youngest daughter of the Dragon King of the Eastern Sea. She had delicate features, was bright and capable, and she pleased her father very much. One day she learned that there was to be a Fish Lantern Festival in the world of men, and wanted to go have a look.

"No," said the Dragon King, stroking his beard. "The human world is very disorderly. It's not the place for a dragon princess like you."

Acting like a spoiled child, Longnu cried and pestered her father. But no matter what she said, the Dragon King would not let her go. Longnu pouted and said to herself, "You won't let me go, but I'll get there for sure." At the second watch she stealthily slipped out of the crystal palace and changed into a beautiful fishergirl. She walked in the moonlight to the place where the Fish Lantern Festival was being held.

It was a small fishing village, on the streets of which were all sorts of fish lanterns: yellow croaker, red snapper, inkfish, lobster, crab, scallop, conch, coral.... Longnu looked now eastward, now westward, and the more she saw, the happier she became. In a short while she squeezed through the crowd to a crossroads, which bustled with such noise and excitement it resembled a sea of colourful lights and lanterns. Infatuated by the scene, Longnu stood there watching in amazement.

Just at that moment, some cold tea came pouring down from the second storey of a pavilion. It fell right on her head, throwing her into great confusion. She did not know what to do. Because she was a young dragon transformed into a girl, any touch of water was sure to change her back into her original shape, but if she changed back on the spot, she would cause a downpour of rain and devastate the Lantern Festival. Squeezing hastily through the crowd, she ran desperately toward the sea. But just as she reached the beach, a deafening crash rent the air and she changed into a huge fish lying in the sand, unable to move.

Soon two young fishermen, one fat and one thin, came along. They were greatly surprised to spot the huge shiny fish lying on the sand. What kind of fish is this, and why has it run aground? they wondered.

"I've never seen such a fish before," said the timid fat man, standing far away from the fish. "It must be inauspicious. Let's go away."

But the bold thin young man refused to go. Touching the fish with his hands, he said, "It doesn't matter what kind of fish it is. If we carry it to the village to sell it on the market, we'll surely make some money."

After discussing it for a while, the two young men carried the huge fish to the market to sell.

That evening Guanyin Bodhisattva was sitting idle in the Purple Bamboo Forest. She saw clearly what had happened, and in her benevolence she said to Shancai beside her, "You go quickly to the market to buy that huge fish, and then release it into the sea."

"But Guanyin Bodhisattva," the boy said and kowtowed, "where do I get the silver to buy it with?"

"You can get a handful from the incense burner," said Guanyin Bodhisattva, smiling.

Shancai nodded and quickly ran to the courtyard to get a handful of incense ashes and, riding a lotus flower, flew to the village market.

In the village market, the two young men were surrounded by people who had come to watch the fish lanterns. Some of them were amazed at the sight of such a huge fish, some admired it, and others inquired about the price. They chattered about it, but none would buy it.

"Young men, the fish is too big to buy; you should cut it into pieces and sell it piece by piece," a white-bearded old man suggested.

The thin young man thought this was a good idea. He went to borrow a knife from a butcher shop and handed it to the fat young man. Seeing the many people standing around him, the fat young man was no longer scared. He raised the knife and was about to kill the fish when suddenly a little boy cried out:

"Look! The fish is shedding tears!"

The fat young man stayed his knife to take a look. Sure enough, the huge fish's two eyes were filled with shiny tears. Scared out of his wits, he dropped the knife and ran to hide in the crowd. But the thin young man, fearing that the money which was almost in his hands might be lost, quickly picked up the knife and made to stab at the fish, but was quickly stopped by a little Buddhist novice, who rushed up and shouted breathlessly:

"Don't kill it! I'll buy it!"

All the onlookers were astonished. Why did a little Buddhist novice want to buy the fish?

The white-bearded old man snorted and said, "A monk wanting to buy fish! Perhaps he'd like to resume a secular life?"

This ironical remark made the little Buddhist novice's face turn red. "I'll buy this fish in order to release it," he said as he fished out some bits of silver to hand to the thin young man. Then he asked them to help carry the fish tô the seaside.

The thin young man inwardly rejoiced: "We can still make money out of this. After the little Buddhist novice has left, we can carry the fish back and sell it again." So he beckoned to the fat young man, and the two of them carried the big fish and followed the little monk to the sea.

Upon arriving at the sea shore, the little monk asked them to put the fish into the water. Once in the water, the big fish splashed and swam away. In the distance it turned back to nod several times to the little monk before disappearing.

After the fish had gone, the thin young man took out the silver and handed it to the fat young man, who started to examine it. But the bits of silver suddenly turned into incense ashes and were blown away by a gust of wind. They turned to look for the little monk, but he had also disappeared.

In the dragon palace of the Eastern Sea, there had been utter confusion after the young princess left. The Dragon King was so worried his beard hairs stood on end, while the turtle prime minister stretched his neck,

the crab general guarding the door spit foam, and the shrimp palace maids knelt on the floor shaking in fear. The farce did not stop until daybreak when the princess returned.

"You wretch!" the Dragon King shouted angrily at his daughter when he saw she was back. "You dared violate the rules of the palace and went out on your own! Where have you been?"

Seeing her father in a rage, Longnu told him the truth: "I went out to watch the Fish Lantern Festival. If not for Guanyin Bodhisattva, who sent Shancai to rescue me, I'd have died long ago." Then she told him the whole story.

The Dragon King felt very sorry on learning of her bitter experience, but fearing that Guanyin Bodhisattva might spread the news and the Jade Emperor would reprimand him for not having been strict with his daughter, he became extremely indignant. In his rage, he drove Longnu out of the crystal palace.

Banished from the palace, Longnu was greatly grieved. Where should she go in the vast Eastern Sea? She wept bitterly as she wandered to the Lotus Ocean. The sound of her weeping reached Purple Bamboo Forest and Guanyin Bodhisattva realized that it was Longnu. She sent Shancai to meet her. Jumping and skipping, Shancai came to Longnu and asked smilingly:

"Don't you recognize me, the little Buddhist novice, Sister Longnu?" Quickly drying her tears, Longnu said bashfully, "You're Brother Shancai, my saviour." With that, she prostrated herself before him to express her gratitude.

Shancai grasped her hand and said, "Guanyin Bodhisattva sent me to meet you here. Let's go to her."

Hand in hand, Shancai and Longnu came to Purple Bamboo Forest. At the sight of Guanyin Bodhisattva sitting cross-legged on the lotus throne, Longnu fell on her knees to kowtow to her. Guanyin Bodhisattva loved the girl very much, and let her live together with Shancai as brother and sister in a nearby cave. Later, the cave was called the Shancai-Longnu Cave.

Longnu became a follower of Guanyin Bodhisattva. The Dragon King often came to ask her to go back with him. But, fascinated by the beautiful scenery of Putuo Mountain, she never returned to the icy crystal palace even once.

Compiled by Zhou Hexing
Translated by Xiong Zhenru

The Nine Dragons and the Tiantai Mountains

PEOPLE say that the Tiantai Mountains were originally a lotus flower with dragon scales, its seventy-two peaks the brilliant petals and the highest Flower Top Peak the stamen of the lotus flower.

A long, long time ago, before the Tiantai Mountains appeared, the place was an endless expanse of water called the Eastern Sea. As some old sayings go, "There are high waves even on a windless day" and "All tigers are heralded by wind, and all dragons by downpours." Every time the Dragon King of the Eastern Sea and his nine sons came out on their mission of bringing rain, there would be a howling hurricane, terrible storms and towering waves on the sea. When fishermen were caught in this onslaught, their boats would capsize and they would drown. So graveyards lined the seashore and there was an incessant wail of mourning. The nine dragon children were, however, all very kind-hearted. Their hearts bled to see so many human beings killed when they summoned clouds and rain.

The youngest of them was very sorry about this. One day it was his turn to be on duty. At the swaying of his tail, there was a peal of thunder and a blinding flash of lightning which sent up an avalanche of billows across the sea. Suddenly he spotted a fishing boat. It was being tossed about by the waves and was on the verge of sinking. The young dragon leapt into mid-air, trying to keep his distance from the water in order to save the boat. But it was too late. He saw the boat hurled against a reef by the raging billows and broken to pieces. In low spirits he went back home.

"Why all this gloom today?" his elder brothers inquired.

"Dear brothers," replied the youngest dragon. "Every time we perform our missions, we stir up high winds and heavy rains on the sea, so that many human beings are killed. Today I overturned another boat."

"There, there, youngest brother, we are carrying out the Jade Emperor's commands to ensure rainfall for people on earth. We can't do anything else."

"We could come up with an innocuous way of carrying out our mission," the youngest dragon said. He didn't get a wink of sleep that night.

Early the next morning he went to his elder brothers with an idea. "What about each of us offering eight scales to be made into a lotus flower? We can put it out on the sea when we are going out as a sort of shelter for the fisherfolk when it storms."

The suggestion was agreed to by the other dragons, whereupon they contributed altogether seventy-two scales, despite the intense pain of pulling them out, to be made into an enormous lotus flower. This was sent drifting out to sea to protect the fisherfolk from the storms.

Somehow the Queen Mother of the West got to know about this, and she longed to possess this rare unearthly treasure. So she had the nine dragons thrown into the

heavenly jail on a trumped-up charge, thus securing the lotus for herself. She had it placed in the lotus pond of her peach orchard.

The fishermen fell victims once again to disasters at sea. The nine dragons, locked up in jail, grieved at the wretched weeping of the fishermen. But try as they might, they couldn't free themselves from their celestial shackles. One day, the golden locks began to clatter, and Red Peach Fairy and Green Peach Fairy, who were in charge of the heavenly jail, went to have a look. They found the youngest dragon having a tantrum.

"Dear fairy sisters, be kind and set us free," he pleaded.

"But we can't," said the two fairy sisters. "We would end up on the gallows for that offence."

"How can you remain unmoved by the suffering of those fishermen down there on earth?"

The two sisters were chastened. Disgusted with the Queen Mother's highhandedness, and moved by the selflessness of the dragons, they decided to set them free and retrieve the lotus flower for the sake of the people on earth. Soon the dragons were flying off to the Eastern Sea with the lotus flower.

Soon afterwards the Queen Mother learned of their escape. Furious, she sent heavenly troops to get the lotus flower back from the dragons. She threatened them with heavy penalties for their disobedience.

The nine dragons entered into a fierce battle with the heavenly forces. It lasted from daybreak to dusk. Heavenly reinforcements only made the nine dragons fight the more desperately.

The Queen Mother, enraged by this audacity, sent a god with a heavenly edict from the Jade Emperor ordering the nine dragons to cease fighting, hand over the lotus flower, and confess their guilt at the heavenly court. When they rejected this order, the god set loose the heavenly edict which, after hovering for some time in mid-air, turned into an enveloping pall and covered the lotus flower up.

The nine dragons rushed to rescue the lotus flower, but were suddenly blinded by a dazzling light. They were captured by the heavenly troops. When they opened their eyes, they found the lotus flower and the sea had disappeared. A mountain in the shape of the lotus flower had emerged, its highest peak like the stamen of a flower surrounded by seventy-two petal-like peaks. These later came to be called the Tiantai Mountains.

The Queen Mother, resenting what the nine dragons and the peach fairies had done, relegated the former to suffer in pools east of the Tiantai Mountains, and the latter to tend magical plants for her in the Peach-Orchard Cave in the mountains.

Nowadays people can still see the nine pools housing the nine dragons up in the Tiantai Mountains.

Compiled by Cao Zhitian
Translated by Li Hong

The Copper Kettle with the Leaky Bottom

ONCE upon a time, there was a small village called Golden Dragon Bend high in the Tiantai Mountains. The soil there was so fertile that a stamp of the foot could squeeze oil out of the ground. With favourable weather, the people there reaped bumper harvests year in and year out, and had a happy life. But the good times did not last. Once it did not rain for almost a year. The fields cracked and became as hard as iron. The people were so hungry that they were only skin and bones. Having no way out, some fled to other places while some hanged themselves.

What caused this disaster?

In a col near Golden Dragon Bend lived a turtle. Relying on his magic power, which he had practised for a thousand years, he made trouble. One night he appeared in the dreams of all the villagers, saying, "From now on, if you supply me with five quintals of rice and a cow, I'll send rain down immediately. Otherwise, I'll let both you and your livestock die."

Next day, all the villagers compared their strange dreams and found they were the same. The cattle were the peasants' treasures, being essential to their lives. But since the turtle was very vicious, they had no way

out but to cook rice and a cow for him.

The turtle immediately gobbled down the sweet rice and tasty beef. Before long, there were only two cows left in the village, and the bottoms of the rice bins could be seen. Some brave young men were enraged and wanted to kill the turtle. They got together to talk over ways and means.

But walls have ears. When the turtle got the news, he stirred up a black wind to blow the lads to him, and then he ate them. He thought to himself evilly, "Tomorrow is the peach banquet given by the Queen Mother of the West. I'll report to the Jade Emperor so that you will have no rain for ten years."

The following day, after arriving at the heavenly palace, the turtle pulled in his neck and said to the Jade Emperor, "Your Majesty, at Golden Dragon Bend in the Tiantai Mountains down on earth the people are very vicious. They have planned secretly not to worship Heaven and Earth, and even blasphemed against Your Majesty!"

Hearing these words, the Jade Emperor was enraged. He immediately ordered the Thunder God and Rain God beside him not to send a drop of rain there for ten years so that the people would all die.

In Golden Dragon Bend there also lived a Little Golden Dragon. Although he was not as magically powerful as the turtle, he was kind and resented the turtle's actions. One day, as he was resting in a cave after some tiring exercise, he suddenly heard cries outside. He leapt into the sky and saw that the villagers of Golden Dragon Bend were weeping. So turning himself into a young man and approaching a weeping old woman, he asked, "What's made you so sad, grandmother?" The old woman told him how the turtle had played his tricks, and how the crops were withering without rain.

Little Golden Dragon fumed with anger. He wanted to tear the turtle into pieces to avenge the villagers. Since he was not powerful enough magically to make rain, he determined to steal the magic rain kettle from the heavenly palace.

Next morning, he rode on a cloud to the Water God Hall, which was guarded vigilantly by two guardian gods, one holding a copper hammer and the other a halberd. Little Golden Dragon had an idea. He turned into a fair, plump boy and walked unhurriedly towards the hall.

"Where do you come from and why are you running about here, boy?" the two gods shouted.

"I'm the Jade Emperor's nephew. Grandma asked me to get the magic kettle to water the peaches," he answered smilingly. But the two gods did not believe him.

"If you don't let me in, fine. I'll go back and tell grandma."

The two gods were worried, for if it was true, their interference with the orders of the Queen Mother of the West could cause trouble. Looking at the boy again, they thought he must be telling the truth, so they let him in.

As soon as Little Golden Dragon got in, he rushed to the treasure house, took a gilded copper kettle and filled it with water, hid it in the breast of his robe and got out of the southern heavenly gate.

He flew directly to Golden Dragon Bend, but just as he got to the sky above the bend, he bumped into the turtle—enemies are bound to meet on a narrow road.

Little Golden Dragon was terribly frightened and his heart sank. He thought, "I'm done for. If he discovers the secret and tells the Jade Emperor, I'll not only not be able to relieve the villagers in Golden Dragon Bend, but also I'll have my head cut off! But there's no use being afraid now. I'll try my best! The people are waiting." Summoning up his courage, he sped by, pretending not to see the turtle.

But the sleek turtle had already caught sight of the dragon from the distance. "Why is he flying so fast?" Then he spotted the bulge in the breast of Little Golden Dragon. "Is there a piece of treasure hidden there?" Just then, a gust of wind blew the dragon's robe up, and the turtle saw the gilded kettle. "How dare you, Little Golden Dragon, steal the treasure from the heavenly palace and send rain down, making trouble for me!" Enraged, he wanted to take Little Golden Dragon and the gilded copper kettle to the Jade Emperor, hoping to get a promotion as a reward. He laughed ferociously, caught at Little Golden Dragon, who had just passed him, and said, "You stole the gilded copper kettle from the heavenly palace. I'll take you to see the Jade Emperor today!"

"How dare you slander me!" Little Golden Dragon retorted.

The turtle started to tear the front part of his robe, but Little Golden Dragon immediately shielded his breast. Then a fight started. But gradually Little Golden Dragon lost his hold. Seeing that the kettle was about to be grabbed away, the dragon had an idea. He heaved it mightily down upon a small hill outside the village. With a terrible crack, the bottom split and clear water flowed out from the seams, down the hill, and towards the fields. The withered crops turned green.

The turtle hurriedly descended to retrieve the kettle, but it seemed to fasten itself to the hill and become a stone kettle. The turtle was so exasperated that he grabbed the dragon and would not let go. They fought desperately in the sky.

The villagers were very angry to see the fight. They beat drums and gongs and cheered for Little Golden Dragon, while burning incense sticks to pray to Heaven. The god on duty received their prayers and reported to the Jade Emperor, who ordered him to investigate the whole situation. After ascertaining the facts, the Jade Emperor jailed the turtle and appointed the dragon the water god of the Tiantai Mountains, in charge of all the dragon pools in the Tiantai area.

Compiled by Cao Xiaobing
Translated by Wu Ling

Dragon-Lions and Dragon Pearls

ON each side of Meridian Gate of the Dragon Pavilion in Kaifeng City once stood a pair of magnificent stone lions. In the mouth of the female lion, under whose paw a young lion played, there was a pearl, said to be the dragon pearl possessed only by dragons. But there was none in the wide-open mouth of the male lion, although he had a ball under his paw. And he glared down at the ground, as if howling in anger.

He was said to be cursing the trickster who stole his dragon pearl. A long time ago, the male lion was the Dragon King of the Yellow River, and had a wife and child. As the Yellow River flooded every year, the Jade Emperor made the dragons door guardians of the emperor in the world of men as punishment for their negligence, planning to allow them to come back to heaven and become dragons again only after three hundred years had passed. So the dragons came down to the human world and the dragon pearls attracted many people, for they were luminous at night and lit nearby places as brightly as if it were day. Many people coveted the pearls. And after 299 years, some bold robbers worked out a cunning plan.

During the Lantern Festival outside the Meridian

Gate, a group of people came along putting on a lion dance. Two golden-maned lions chased a boy, trying to snatch the ball in his hand. But the boy was so nimble that the lions could not get the ball. "How silly they are!" the male dragon-lion thought. After a moment the boy danced in front of the dragon-lion and waved the ball before his eyes. "I'll get it!" the male dragon-lion said to himself. Seizing his opportunity, he opened his mouth and bit right on the ball, but the dragon pearl fell from his mouth. The boy snatched up the pearl and ran away. The dragon-lion, unable to leave his post, could only howl angrily as he helplessly watched his pearl being taken away.

When the three hundred years were up, the male dragon-lion could not turn back into a dragon, because he had lost the pearl. The female dragon-lion had to stay on to accompany her careless husband. Even today, the regretful stone lion still opens its mouth in anger, cursing the tricksters of the world!

Compiled by Gen Chen
Translated by Wu Ling

The Yanyu Herb and the Greedy Dragon

IN Qutang Gorge in Sichuan stood the towering Chijia Mountain, with a cliff fiery red as if hewn out by choppers and knives. It was also called Peach Mountain; this was because it had a peak the shape of a big peach sitting on a huge jade plate formed by clouds circling around it. A cave below the peach, deep and unfathomable, where stalactites hung down and quaint stones jutted from the ground, was called Seven Gates for the number of gates it had. It was a deserted place frequented by beasts of prey. One day a fisherman called Xia Zhongjiao, fleeing from famine and finding refuge here, chased away the animals and settled down at Seven Gates. Making a living by fishing, Xia planted herbs on Yanyu Shoal in the Kuimen River, herbs which brought the dying back to life. He often cured the fishermen living along the Three Gorges of the Yangtze River with the Yanyu herb.

One day a dragon which had been locked up by Yu the Great in Dragon-Confinement Cave under Yanyu Shoal when Yu harnessed the water thousands of years ago slipped out of a ring confining it to the cave. With a whish of its tail it wiped away all the Yanyu herbs. When Xia returned from fishing one day to pick some herbs, he found them all gone. He was wondering what had happened when suddenly a wind arose and waves began to roll. With a crash of thunder, a single-horned dragon emerged from under Yanyu Shoal. Realizing it was the dragon people had told him about, he demanded fearlessly, "Did you take my herbs, you impertinent dragon?"

"What if I did?" sneered the dragon. "I want to take you too. Yu the Great locked me up for thousands of years. I'm hungry. I'll make you my first meal."

The dragon raised its claws and made for Xia Zhongjiao, who jumped into the rolling waves and fought the dragon with his fish trident for three days and nights. On the fourth day, the aging Xia Zhongjiao, his strength failing because of hunger and fatigue, was finally gobbled up by the dragon.

Xia's old wife, overcome with grief at the news of his death, exhorted her son to train himself in aquatic skills in order to avenge his father when he grew up.

Determined to avenge his father, Xia Xiaojiao trained hard while fishing to support his mother. After a few years, he became as tall and stout as his father, and was able to tread water fiercely, submerge for seven days and nights and fight with a fish trident. One day, coming home from fishing, he became anxious at not seeing his mother coming out to meet him. He went home only to see his mother at her last breath. He was just going to fetch a doctor when his mother tugged at his sleeve and told him in a laboured voice, "I can only be saved by the Yanyu herb your father grew, my son."

New hatred added to his old grudge, Xiaojiao took leave of his mother. Fish trident in hand, he made for Yanyu Shoal, where he shouted at the top of his voice,

"Listen to me, you greedy dragon. Give me the magic Yanyu herb or I'll cut you in pieces."

With a crash of thunder, the dragon emerged from its cave and gloated, "Good. You'll be my next meal." He swooped down on Xia Xiaojiao who, with a movement quick as lightning, stuck his fish trident into the stomach of the greedy dragon, bringing out a spurt of black blood.

The dragon, fiercer because of the wound, fought the young man who was the braver for his hatred. After seven days and nights, the dragon, weakened by loss of blood, turned and fled into its cave. It slammed the door with a swish of its tail. No matter how Xiaojiao rammed the door, breaking his trident in his effort, he could not open it. At his wits' end, he had to go home. Finding his mother deteriorating, he thought hard about a way to open the stone door of the dragon's cave.

At midnight, Xiaojiao saw in his dreams an old man emerging from the peach peak of Chijia Mountain, riding a cluster of clouds and holding a golden book in his hand. "You are a brave young fisherman who has lived up to your mother's expectations, Xiaojiao. Take this book and read Yu the Great's tactics for subduing a dragon."

Xiaojiao accepted the book. "Who are you, granddad?" he asked.

"I'm your neighbour, Sage Peach. The book only tells you a few treasures. It is your wit and courage and the skill in using these treasures that will help you." After saying this, the old man stepped on to the cluster of clouds and floated away.

Awakened by the cocks' crowing, Xiaojiao rubbed

his eyes and, remembering his dream, saw in his hands a golden book. He lit a pine torch and read it, keeping in mind what was said in the book. Without waiting for daybreak to bid his mother goodbye, he jumped into the river and came to the dragon's cave under Yanyu Shoal, where he moved away a slab of stone and produced a stone cap, which he put on his head. The cave door gave way at the first blow of his stone hat. He groped in the pitch-dark cave, unable to see a thing until he found a stone box. From it he produced a pair of stone boots. When he stepped into them, the boots carried him to the second door, inside which was a stone horse. At sight of Xiaojiao, the horse pricked up its ears and neighed. Xiaojiao pulled two swords out of its ears and in their glittering cool light saw the characters "Yu the Great's Sword" on the hilts. Then the stone boots carried him to the third door, behind which the greedy dragon rested on a stone platform.

Opening its eyes and seeing Xiaojiao, the dragon leapt up, defending the platform from Xiaojiao. His swords were too short to reach the dragon on the platform, but Xiaojiao came up with an idea. He pretended to retreat. The dragon at once chased after him, not wanting to give up this delicious morsel. Xiaojiao halted abruptly, leapt onto the stone platform, raised his swords, slashed the platform open and discovered a ring. He tossed the ring over the dragon's head, confining it to the cave. Behind the platform he found the Yanyu herb. On his way out he took three stone padlocks from the stone horse's back and locked the three doors with them. The greedy dragon could not come out to harm people any more.

Xiaojiao returned home with the Yanyu herb. As a

day in the dragon's cave equals a year on land, when he arrived home, his mother had been dead for a long time. He buried his mother and planted the Yanyu herb and, like his father, treated the fishermen all his life.

Compiled by Lai Cenglin
Translated by Yu Fanqin

Carving Dragons

LONG, long ago, at Qingming Festival, the carpenters who made their living outside their home villages all came back for spring ploughing. One of them was Master Yang of Dongxiang Village, whose given name was unknown. Superbly skilled, he could carve dragons, draw phoenixes and build compounds with five courtyards and large houses, and high arches with big eaves. With his son Qijin behind him, Master Yang carried his bedroll slung over his back and his carpenter tools and a little cooking pot on a shoulder pole. One day they came to the Dragon Pool in Louyi Village near Dali.

In those years, a cruel swine dragon with a pitch-black body lived in this ghastly and bloodcurdling pool. Every three years, at dusk on the 24th of the sixth lunar month, the dragon would cover the sun with dark clouds and cause a terrible tempest. Floods would wash away the bridges and houses, turning the fields for several hundred li around into waste land. The swine dragon would rush through the flood waters towards Erhai Lake, stirring up waves as high as hills, wrecking boats and swallowing fish and turtles. After making trouble for a whole day and night, it would return, bringing thunderstorms. These disasters forced the Bai people to flee to Mount Cangshan and eat grass roots and tree bark. Only after the swine dragon quieted down could they come back home to look after their fields and rebuild their houses. The people living in the village never had a peaceful life.

Strangely, the swine dragon in the pool could not bear to see any iron or copper ware. If somebody fetched water from the pool with a metal container, the dragon would stretch out a claw to drag him into the pool and eat him. After many years, thick woods grew around the pool, hiding it completely. Even the wind could not blow in.

That day, as Master Yang and his son Qijin hastened along, the weather was terribly hot. Qijin wanted to drink water to quench his thirst, but could not see any about. Seeing the gloomy thick forest, he put down the shoulder pole, took the copper pot and rushed to the pool. Master Yang ran after him to warn him not to fetch the water. But Qijin only turned his head back, saying "I'm thirsty, dad," and then went into the forest.

Everything happened quickly. Just as Qijin had knelt down on one knee and dipped his pot into the water, black smoke rose from the pool, followed by a claw which hooked on to the copper pot and dragged the boy into the water. Then there came a terrible clap of thunder and a shower of hail. When Master Yang arrived, he found only one of his son's straw sandals, left on the bank.

Qijin, thirteen years old, was Master Yang's only son and had travelled everywhere with him. Now that he had suddenly disappeared in bright daylight so near to his home village, Master Yang felt desperately sad. He wanted to jump into the water to fight the evil dragon, but knew it would be no use. Unsure what to do, he stared dully at the straw sandal and cried bitterly, leaving only when the sun set.

An old woman passing by saw the baggage and the carpenter tools by the side of the road. Following the sound of the crying, she found Master Yang in the woods. After hearing his story, she persuaded him to go back to the village with her first and then think what they could do about it. By this time, the villagers were suffering from a flood, living in straw huts on the hills. Although they were having a hard time themselves, they showed their sympathy for Master Yang and came to comfort him. A boy called Treasure and a girl called Phoenix were especially friendly to him. They gave him water to drink and massaged his back. The sight of these two warmhearted children made Master Yang even sadder. The villagers persuaded him to rest for two days, planning to send people to accompany him back home.

Being too sad to eat and sleep, Master Yang only stared at the straw sandal. The next day, he decided not to stay on to fight against the swine dragon to revenge his son. As he was skilled in carving dragons and painting phoenixes and remembered some sacred incantations from the "Wood Scripture",* he decided he would instead carve and paint a wooden dragon, bring it to life by chanting the sacred incantation and send it into the pool on an auspicious day to fight the swine

*The "Wood Scripture" was said to be an architectural scripture handed down from the legendary carpenter Lu Ban, but in fact was a collection of architectural experience originally handed down orally. Bai carpenters in Jianchuan chanted the sacred scripture to ward off disasters, in addition to their usual work building houses, carving Buddhist statues and painting walls.

dragon until the evil beast was killed.

When he told his idea to the villagers and discussed it with them, they were only half convinced. However, since they sympathized with him and believed in his skills, they supplied him with food and helped him get wood from the Cangshan Mountains.

He chose an ancient pine tree on a hill, felled it and carried it back with the others, then set up a shed with pine boughs. After offering sacrifices and taking a bath, he started to carve. The two children, Treasure and Phoenix, helped him with cooking, fetching water and passing tools, and the villagers often visited him in their spare time.

Inspired and helped by the villagers, he worked day and night, determined to finish the work and send the dragon into the pool before noon on the 24th of the sixth month. In the final few days, he worked even harder, and many villagers came to light torches for him.

One day, a short, fat stranger came into the shed wearing a black felt cap which made him look like an idler. He folded his arms and squatted down beside the stove to watch Master Yang work in silence.

"What do you want, brother?" Master Yang asked him.

The stranger did not reply. He took out something from under his cape and held it to Master Yang.

"Fish?" Master Yang was puzzled.

"Brother carpenter," the stranger said, "I've heard that you have superb skills. May I trouble you to bring this fish back to life?" So saying, he handed it over to Master Yang.

Master Yang took a look. It was a dried fish. Placing

it on a pile of wood shavings, he made an obeisance to it by putting two hands before his chest, saying, "How can I be said to have such ability?"

"You really can't?"

"I really can't."

"How can you make a wooden dragon come alive then, if you can't bring a fish back to life?" the stranger muttered as he left the shed without a word of farewell.

Master Yang did not see the stranger's face clearly, only hearing his muffled laughter. He was about to follow him out when a sudden sound came from behind. Turning around, he saw the dried fish moving on the pile of shavings. Quickly realizing what it was up to, he threw his axe at the fish, which wriggled effortlessly into the pile of shavings. Treasure, Phoenix and the villagers all came to look for the fish but failed.

Everybody knew who had played this trick!

Master Yang spread rice around the shed* and asked the two children to keep watch. After that nothing happened. Maybe the swine dragon had only come to jeer at him, and then gone back to sleep in the pool.

At noon on June 24th, Master Yang completed his wooden dragon and laid it on an open spot of ground. Because the swine dragon was black, he painted his wooden dragon with white clay until it was silvery white, and hung red ribbons on its horns. The villagers came to congratulate him. At three o'clock in the afternoon, Master Yang bit his middle finger and had the dragon's eyes, nose, mouth and ears painted with

---

*In the past people took rice, salt, iron, suger and tea as the "five treasures", among which rice was the most important. When people camped in the hills, they would spread rice around the place to ward off devils, tigers and leopards.

his own blood. While painting, he chanted incantations and prayed to Lu Ban, the earliest ancestor of carpenters, to guarantee his victory.

At sunset, people lit torches, sang Bai folk songs and beat drums and gongs as they carried the wooden dragon down the hill. Master Yang, holding a torch high, with Treasure and Phoenix on each side, marched in the vanguard. When they came to the pool, he asked the villagers to put the torches around it. Then he clenched his fists, drew some magic figures, chanted the sacred scriptures, then sent the wooden dragon into the pool.

As soon as the ceremony was over, he led the people back up the hill, for the pool would soon be a battlefield.

Before they reached the hill top, a peal of thunder was heard. Two clouds soared into the sky, the white one in the front, the black one behind. Amidst a tempest the two dragons started to fight.

Master Yang and the villagers anxiously watched the fight from the top of the hill. The white dragon was nimble, flying vigorously through the clouds, but the black dragon was often clumsy and in a defensive position. In the torrential rain, Master Yang and the villagers cheered for the white dragon as they watched.

The two dragons fought from the south to the north, but neither side would give in. After a while, the smaller white dragon gradually could not stand its ground and started to beat a retreat while battling on. The black dragon tried to spray dark clouds to shroud the white dragon, and the white dragon could only bare its claws weakly.

Seeing this, Master Yang loosened his hair and started praying for the earliest ancestor's protection, and the people began to beat drums and gongs to cheer the white dragon up. But no matter what they did, the white dragon could not withstand the onslaughts from the black dragon. It retreated to Mount Cangshan, and its scales were scattered all over the ground. The black dragon, not letting up, continued to chase after it. Finally the white dragon was torn into pieces, and a dark cloud covered the sky while a flood appeared on the land.

However, the white dragon's defeat did not make the villagers lose confidence in Master Yang. He drew a line on the ground, indicating that he would not cross the line to go back home until he vanquished the swine dragon. He decided to collect wood on Mount Cangshan alone, but the villagers would not let him. They said that if he wanted wood, they would go with him, and if he wanted to carve a dragon again, they would supply him with food as usual. They would wait for the next 24th of the sixth month and fight again with the evil dragon.

Now the villagers' life was even more miserable. The rainstorm, which had lasted the whole night, had washed the houses and crops away. There was only water as far as the eye could see. The villagers were so indignant that they set off to fetch wood that very day, leaving only Treasure and Phoenix behind.

Master Yang took his son's straw sandal with him and gazed at it as he walked with the villagers toward the mountain. On his way he met Blacksmith Master Zhao. After hearing his story, Master Zhao was willing to help. Master Zhao concluded that the white dragon's defeat was due to its lack of iron scales, teeth and claws and said he would help armour the wooden dragon. His suggestion enlightened Master Yang. But where could he get enough iron and people to do it?

Master Zhao said he would ask the miners from Mount Fengyu to send iron, the blacksmiths from Heqing to make the iron scales, and the carpenters from Jianchuan to help carve the wooden dragon. But Master Yang insisted that he do the carving himself.

"Take it easy, brother!" Master Zhao said and left. In the meanwhile Master Yang and the villagers went up into the mountains for wood.

Treasure and Phoenix collected materials, set up a new hut for Master Yang and picked up some fish and shrimps left on the land when the flood receded to assuage their hunger. When the weather turned fine, they ploughed the fields and sowed some late buckwheat while waiting for the others to return.

One day an old woman with a Jianchuan accent came along. At first Treasure and Phoenix thought she must be going to a fair in Dali, but actually she had come to see Master Yang. She said she was Master Yang's sister-in-law and had come especially when she learned he was carving a dragon for revenge, bringing a bag of food and a steel axe handed down from the family ancestors to help him. Since he was not at home, she asked to leave the things in his hut and go to the fair in Dali, saying she would visit Yang on her way back. Before leaving, she gave the children two sweet and fragrant Jianchuan pears. The children hid the bag and axe in the straw in the hut, and buried the pears in ashes.

Two days later Master Yang and the villagers returned. They had cut down an ancient pine tree for carving the dragon and some materials for the rebuilding of houses. Although they had suffered for a month, they were still in high spirits. When Master Yang entered the hut, Treasure and Phoenix handed the bag, the axe and the two pears to him and told him where they had come from.

"I have no sister-in-law!" He was puzzled.

The two children described the old woman's appearance, accent and look, even the Jianchuan bamboo basket on her back. But Master Yang kept shaking his head. He looked at the axe; it had a thick back and thin edge. It was indeed a good axe. But as he examined it more closely, the handle suddenly began to move in his hand and instantly twined around his arm. The axe had turned into a snake! Its bloody mouth open wide, its tongue out, it made as if to attack his breast.

The two children cried out in dismay. Seeing the axe turn into a poisonous snake, Master Yang calmly strangled it. When the snake no longer moved, he snapped it vigorously through the air. The snake's bones all broke and its joints became loose. Then Master Yang threw the body into the stove, where it sizzled on the fire.

The two children hurriedly opened the old woman's bag. Seeing what was inside it, Master Yang's face turned blue with anger. They were all wood chips—the scales, claws and bones of the white dragon. And the two pears had turned into poisonous jack-in-the-pulpits. It was another trick of the swine dragon to murder Master Yang and the two children.

A month later, the villagers set up new huts on Mount Cangshan. They opened up wasteland to sow late buckwheat and turnips, so as to tide over the lean year. Master Yang started to carve a dragon again, and Master Zhao and other blacksmiths came to cast iron to make scales, teeth and claws.

Treasure learned skills from Blacksmith Zhao and Phoenix from Carpenter Yang. Before long, Phoenix produced a small wooden dragon which the boy armed with iron teeth and claws. Seeing the life-like small dragon, both Master Yang and Master Zhao were very pleased, and formally accepted the two children as their apprentices.

Just then an old white-haired monk wrapped in a blanket came begging with a rattle-drum in his hand, a black dog trotting behind him. At that time the Bai people all believed in Buddhism and would donate whenever they saw a monk. They invited him in and gave him wine and food. As it was dark and raining, Master Yang invited the monk to stay the night.

But who would have guessed that at midnight, when everyone was sound asleep, the monk would rise stealthily, tear the small dragon into pieces, set the hut on fire and send the black dog to attack Master Yang? Just as the dog was about to bite Master Yang's throat, Treasure woke up and smashed its head with a spade. Phoenix also woke up and threw an axe at the monk, cutting one of his fingers off. The monk ran away in a gale of wind. By the time the villagers rushed over, the monk and the dog were nowhere to be seen. From then on, they became more vigilant, keeping watch day and night in case the swine dragon should come again after its wound was healed.

By noon on the 24th of the sixth month, a new wooden dragon had been carved and armoured. The awesome dragon, as bright as silver, was surrounded by eight small dragons made by Treasure and Phoenix.

At dusk, torches were lit, and people singing songs and beating drums and gongs carried the nine dragons down Mount Cangshan and sent them into the pool. After a ceremony, Master Yang led the people back up the hill. But before they could climb far, thunder came from the pool and a black cloud flew into the sky, followed by nine white clouds. The white dragons, one big one and eight small ones, surrounded the black dragon as they fought. Master Yang, Master Zhao and the villagers stood on the hilltop to watch, beating drums and gongs and cheering.

The dragons fought from south to north. The vast sky became a battlefield. Harassed by the nine white dragons, the black dragon, though big and strong, gradually became exhausted and its black scales, big as dustpans, began to fall off one after another. Struggling desperately, swinging its thick tail, it tried to sweep the small white dragons into the lake.

Seeing that the white dragons were gaining the upper hand, Master Yang and the villagers waved their axes, saws, hammers, hoes and sickles and cheered for them.

When the fight came roaring back down from the north, the black dragon's head was lolling downward. The white clouds occupied the whole sky while the black cloud, looking like a small blanket, was pressed downward, and before long it sank into the lake.

The rain stopped and white clouds covered the whole village. A bright moon rose in the sky. The big white dragon, with Qijin riding on its back, flew westward, followed by the eight small dragons. Master Yang and the others cried and cheered. When the white dragons reached the sky above the pool, they split the thick forest with nine claps of thunder and plunged into the depths of the pool.

From then on, the swine dragon pool became the white dragon pool. Sunlight came in though the breaks in the forest, and the water of the pool became clear. In order to commemorate Master Yang and the white dragons, people built a white dragon temple, with Master Yang's statue sitting in the middle, flanked by those of Treasure and Phoenix. On the board of the temple was the big white dragon and around its eight columns curled the eight small dragons. In the season for transplanting rice seedlings, people often found the dragon's bodies covered by grass: this was the grass caught on the dragon's bodies on their way to bring down rain during the night. The villagers also remembered Master Zhao and enshrined him in a side room with a hammer in his hand.

The evil swine dragon was imprisoned at the bottom of Erhai Lake. He wanted to come out every 24th of the sixth month in the evening, but dared not. Because torches were lit everywhere in the village that evening, he thought the villagers must be carving wooden dragons again.

Translated by Wu Ling

The Dragon Tablet

ONCE upon a time in a village near Kunming lived an old man named Ma Yingsheng and his wife.

Though the old couple had been married for more than thirty years, they had no children. How eagerly they hoped for a son or a daughter!

"Merciful lord! Give us a child," the old couple prayed every day.

One year, the old woman suddenly got pregnant. How happy the old couple were! However, a year passed by with no child. And then another year passed. The old man sighed: "It must be a disease giving you this big belly. How can a woman be pregnant for two years?"

In the third year, a child was born. The old couple were so happy they cried. But the boy was born in a drought year, so the old man named him Ganhan, meaning "born in a year of drought".

Ganhan was able to walk only two months after his birth. By the third month he could talk, and at only six months he was able to climb the mountain to pick mushrooms and collect firewood with his mother.

There wasn't a drop of rain for two years after Ganhan was born. Crops wouldn't grow in the fields, so the farmers had to look for bark and grass roots to eat.

One day, Ganhan asked his mother: "Why don't people grow rice to feed themselves?"

"My child, the Dragon King doesn't make rain. How can they grow rice?"

"Mother, I shall find the Dragon King!"

"My child, the Dragon King lives in his palace. Only good swimmers can go there."

Thereafter, Ganhan went to Black Dragon Pool to practise swimming every day. No matter if it was cold or hot, he went to practise. He sought the dragon palace every day.

The dragon palace was very deep. One day, two days ... a month elapsed, but Ganhan couldn't find it. Two months went by, but still no palace. He kept seeking it for a hundred days.

One day, Ganhan was so tired that he dozed off in the water. Soon after he closed his eyes, he found himself inside a transparent, well-lit palace. A beautiful princess walked slowly out from the inner court of the palace. She wore a dress made of coral and a pair of shoes made of pearls and agates. The light glowing from her eyes onto her bright face was as cool and beautiful as autumn moonlight.

As Ganhan stared in surprise at the princess, she spoke:

"Ganhan, to find the dragon palace, you should look for the dragon cave first. Now the Dragon King is still sleeping; you must hurry!" The princess's voice was as clear and melodious as a stroke on a crystal glass. Every word had the sound of a rolling pearl.

The princess also told the young man how to find the Dragon King. But a wave rose before she had finished speaking, and she turned and ran away. Ganhan hurriedly followed, and to his dismay floated to the surface of the water. He woke up. Having inhaled deeply, he searched along the way the princess had directed him. There he discovered a hole wider than a man's height and swam into it. It was pitch dark inside and the water was icy cold. Grinding his teeth, he felt his way down in a spiral. Everywhere he touched there were pointed rocks as sharp as knives. At last, he reached the bottom of the hole and found two doors, tightly shut, with thorns all over them.

Ganhan pushed on the doors with his hands until they were thoroughly scratched. He kicked them with his feet until his feet were lacerated. He tried his body, but the thorns pierced it. For a day and a night he tried to open the doors, but they were still tightly shut. His hands and feet were injured so badly that they dripped with blood.

"Ganhan!" the princess's whisper sounded in his ear, "if you want to open the doors, get the dragon tablet quickly."

Ganhan had to leave the cave and head back to the mountain, where he picked some medicinal herbs and applied them to his wounds. Then he went back home.

"Where is the dragon tablet?" he asked his mother.

"The dragon tablet is in the Muslim mosque, my child!"

Ganhan went to the mosque right away.

It was a day of worship that day. All the Muslims had gathered to pray for rain. They had been discussing for forty days but could not find a person who could plant the dragon tablet.

"I have come to fetch the dragon tablet," said Ganhan as he greeted the imam.

"Excellent!" the imam replied. "What's your name? Can you swim?"

"My name is Ganhan. I can not only swim but also sleep in the water!"

"Oh, thank Allah! We've got someone to plant the dragon tablet!" cried the imam happily.

All the people there clasped their hands in prayer and Ganhan prayed with them.

Since the person to plant the dragon tablet was at long last found, the congregation began to move. They took off their headcoverings and shoes, held incense in their hands, and prayed. An imam held up the dragon tablet with both hands. Ganhan followed the group to Black Dragon Pool, where the imam handed him the dragon tablet. As soon as he got the tablet he dived into the water so hurriedly that he had no time to take off his clothes. Feeling his way into the dragon cave, he knocked on the doors with the tablet. Instantly the thorn-covered door opened, and Ganhan walked into the brightly-lit dragon palace. Soft music played as the Dragon King, clad in a black gown, slept there with a blood-red pearl held loosely in his mouth. Remembering what the princess had told him, Ganhan rushed to grab the pearl, put it into his mouth and swallowed it.

The Black Dragon King awoke. Breathing fire from his mouth and nose, he shouted: "Who has stolen my pearl?"

"I have swallowed it!" replied Ganhan.

The Dragon King jumped up in a rage and snatched a sword. With a vicious snarl, he said, "Give me back my pearl. Quickly, or I will chop you into eight pieces!"

"Black muddle-head, you've starved too many people to death! This day next year will be the anniversary of your death. Die!" As he spoke, Ganhan raised the dragon tablet high and struck the Dragon King to the ground with one blow. The second blow flattened the dragon's horns. The third removed the dragon's head.

The Dragon King died. Ganhan changed into a dragon himself and flew out of the cave. Rain began to pour down all over the land.

Compiled by Wang Dong
Translated by Wu Jingchao

A Dragon and Phoenix Match

THIS story happened long, long ago when there were neither dragons nor phoenixes in the world.

In a distant land, a childless old couple led a very lonely and wretched life. They wished not for clothing or food, but for a child. Day after day, the wife went to Seven Stars Hall to worship the God of the Seven Stars. Before she went she would change into clean clothing and then go to the lower stream to wash her feet, the middle stream to wash her body, and the upper stream to wash her hair. Then she would kneel down in Seven Stars Hall and pray: "Oh, benevolent God of the Seven Stars, the Big Dipper. Please give me a child."

After praying for three months and ten days until her lips were worn out and her knees hurt, the old woman did conceive. All day long, the faces of the old couple were wreathed in smiles. They even broke into laughter in their sleep. The old man said, "The God of the Seven Stars is really benevolent. He is sure to give us a chubby son. We'll have grandsons too."

The old woman countered: "As the saying goes, a good daughter is better than a bad son. Provided that we can be parents, I don't mind if it's a boy or a girl."

One day ten months later, her hands holding her abdomen, the old woman cried with pain. Soon after she gave birth. But the old couple were startled to find that she had not given birth to a baby, but a tiny long snake with golden scales and wings. Tears rolling down his face, the old man said, "It's all my bad fortune. We won't have a son in this life. For all our longing, we got this monster. Let's throw it away."

Also shedding tears, the old woman said, "No matter what it may be, it is our flesh and blood. We mustn't desert it. Let's keep it."

Odd as it may seem, the little snake writhed, calling sweetly, "Dad! Mom!" Hearing themselves thus addressed for the first time in their lives, the old couple were so pleased that they took the little snake in their hands.

The little snake continued: "Don't lose heart, father and mother. Although I'm a snake, I can still be a good son to you." So they kept the little snake. He was ugly, but he talked like an adult, and the house was filled with talk and laughter.

Across the yard lived the Piaos, a wealthy family on good terms with the old couple. The Piaos had three daughters. The eldest was ugly, the second was cunning, and the third was beautiful and kind. The three daughters all came over to see the new baby. On entering, they asked, "Let us see your baby, aunty." The old woman lifted up a corner of the coverlet and there crouched a little snake with golden scales and wings.

"Oh dear!" exclaimed the three girls.

"How can a human being give birth to such a creature?" sniffed the eldest daughter.

"My, it gives me goose bumps," commented the second, her hands covering her face.

But the third daughter said with a smile, "Well, well, aunty is a lucky person to give birth to a dragon prince." The old woman's fury at what the eldest and second daughters had said was half dispelled by the praise of the third daughter.

Perhaps the third daughter's praise had gone straight to the heart of the snake, for he begged his parents: "You've had a hard life, father and mother. You ought to have a daughter-in-law now. Please go and ask for the hand of the third daughter as my wife."

"Do not think so highly of yourself, my child," said the old man, knocking out his pipe. "Who'd marry an ugly thing like you?"

"I know your aspirations, my child," said the old woman with a sigh. "But one can only have a good daughter-in-law when one has a good son. How can I approach them and say that my son the snake would like to marry one of their daughters?"

"Please do this one thing for me, mother," the snake pleaded. "I know that the kind-hearted third daughter will marry me."

The snake's eagerness made the old woman agree to go on this errand. But at the Piaos, sitting before the old man and his wife, she was too embarrassed to broach the subject. All she did was scratch the mat on the *kang* with her fingernails. So her first trip achieved nothing.

"Is the marriage arranged?" the snake asked as soon as she returned.

"No."

"But why? Did she refuse?"

"No. I was too embarrassed to propose the match."

"Please go again," the little snake pleaded. "I'll be

resigned if the third daughter says she won't do it."

The following day, the old woman braced herself to make another attempt. But once at the Piaos, remembering how ugly her son was, she couldn't speak out although the proposal was turning over and over on her tongue. All she did was scratch and finger the *kang* mat.

"Well, how about it?" asked the snake when she returned.

"Nothing doing."

"Why not? Did her parents refuse?"

"No. I was too embarrassed to speak up."

The little snake was upset. "If you think I am too ugly to find a wife, I'll return to your belly."

The old woman quickly consoled him. "Don't be mad. I'll definitely speak tomorrow."

The third day, the old woman called again on the Piaos. Though she had made up her mind to speak out, once seated before the Piaos she swallowed her proposal and proceeded to scratch and finger the *kang* mat again.

All three daughters came out of their room.

"How do you have the nerve to call on people when you have a monster for a son?" demanded the first daughter in a shrill voice.

"This old diehard of a woman does nothing but scratch our mat when she comes. Will you give us a new one if you make a hole in it?" added the second daughter.

But the third daughter was kinder. She said softly, "You must have something on your mind, aunty. Do you want to borrow some food or clothing? Please do not hesitate to speak up."

The old woman told them how, after the third daughter's remark about her son the other day, the little snake wished to marry her.

Father Piao was enraged. He shouted at his third daughter, "What a shameless hussy! Speaking whatever nonsense you like! How can you say he's a dragon prince when he's nothing but a snake?"

The third daughter answered slowly, making every word very clear, "It was not nonsense. I think he really *is* a dragon prince."

Piao was incensed. "You dare to talk back, you shameless hussy? Very well, marry him if he is so good."

He had meant to stop her nonsense, but the girl answered, "I'm willing to do just that."

The old man choked with fury.

"You're crazy," said her eldest sister. "You can pick and choose, with your good looks. Why marry a snake?"

"What a great fool," scolded her second sister, "to want to marry a little snake."

Her mother said, "You've refused so many young men from rich families. Why marry an ugly snake who gives people goose flesh? That'll never do."

The old man was in a dilemma. The third daughter had said she was willing. But how could he give such a flower of a daughter to a snake? After much pondering, he had an idea.

"Since time immemorial, all marriages have been arranged by the parents. Although my third daughter has given her consent, I've two conditions. I would ask your magic son to get me two things. If he can do that I'll give him my daughter's hand."

"What are they?"

"First, I want an egg with bones inside."

The old woman returned home very worried. "How did it go?" asked the snake.

"Still no result."

"Why?"

"The third daughter gave her consent," the old woman told him. "But her father said you must do two things to gain his daughter."

"What are they?"

"The first thing is, you must give him an egg with bones inside. All the eggs in the world have a yolk and a white. How can there be bones? He is giving us a hard nut to crack. I think you had better give up."

The little snake laughed and said, "This is as easy as asking a toad to eat a fly or sticking a needle in a cucumber."

"How so?"

"Will you give me an egg?" She gave him an egg which he put on the warm *kang*. Then he coiled himself around it for a month and ten days.

One day, he said to his mother, "Could you take this egg with bones inside to the girl's family?" Only then did his mother realize what he had been doing.

Father Piao was secretly pleased at having frightened the snake away. He was really surprised when the snake's mother brought him an egg. He took the egg and found it looked just like an ordinary egg. So he asked, "How do you know this egg has bones inside, little snake's mother?"

"I don't know, but my son told me so."

Just then the egg shell cracked and a chick poked its head out, chirping. Only then did it dawn on Father

Piao what had happened. He stuck his thumb up in praise of the little snake's cleverness.

His two elder daughters were furious, but the third was extremely pleased. Since his first plan was foiled, Father Piao told the snake's mother, "The second thing I want him to bring me is a bowl of ten li soup."

Again the old woman returned home very worried.

"What's worrying you this time, mother?" asked the snake.

"The old man wanted ten li soup. There's all kinds of soups in this world, but who's ever heard of ten li soup? He was making it difficult for us on purpose." But the little snake laughed.

"What are you laughing at?" asked his mother.

"Well, his two conditions are too simple. Ten li soup is too easy. You wait, I'll go out and return in just a little while." Where was he going? Once outside the door, the snake swished off towards a big pool. He waited beside it with his head in the air.

He was waiting for aully*. Soon a flock of honking ducks flew over and the little snake opened his mouth to let out a gust of white steam, which wrapped around two of the aully and made them flop down before him. With the necks of the birds in his mouth, the little snake swished home.

At sight of the ducks, his mother demanded, "Why did you catch those?"

"Don't ask why, but please make a soup with them." Soon the soup was made, and the little snake asked his mother to invite Father Piao over. When Father Piao sat down at the table, the little snake's mother served

---

*Aully in Korean is duck. It has the same pronounciation as "five li".

him a bowl of aully soup.

The old man asked in a huff, "You call this ten li soup?"

Coiling on the table, the little snake spoke up: "Please think for yourself. One aully means five li. Aren't two of them ten li?"

The old man stared hard, unable to say a word.

As the saying goes, "Sprinkled rice can be picked up, but words said cannot be taken back." The old man accepted his defeat and had to marry his third daughter to the little snake. The night of their wedding, the snake bridegroom said to his bride, "Will you close your eyes?" The bride complied. After a while, he told her, "Now you can open your eyes." The third daughter opened her eyes and saw before her a charming young man. Unable to believe what she saw, the third daughter took her husband's hand, looked at him closely and touched him again and again. She danced with happiness.

The young couple danced for a while and the bride asked her groom, "You were a snake. How did you become a man?"

"I am the son of the Dragon King," he told her. "The old man and woman wanted a son so badly, and besides the ruling king has no son to take over his throne. So my father bade me come to the world of men. Tomorrow I'll go to the capital to sit for the imperial examinations. If I pass the exam as First Scholar, the old king will make me his successor and you'll be queen."

He gave the skin he had shed to the third daughter and told her, "You must never let anyone see the skin on any account. If the skin is burned, I shall die." The saying has it that birds can hear what is said in the daytime, while rats can hear what is said in the night. As the third daughter's two sisters were eavesdropping, they heard everything and were filled with burning jealousy.

Before dawn the following day, the bridegroom left for the capital. Every day the two elder sisters came to ask the third daughter where her bridegroom had gone and whether he had left a snakeskin. Remembering what her husband had told her, she said nothing. But the two sisters would not give up. They asked to stay the night on the pretext of keeping her company. Actually, they wanted to harm her. So the third sister kept the snakeskin in her bosom, not letting go of it for one minute.

One night, when the third sister fell asleep, the eldest sister pinned her down while the second sister pulled out the snakeskin and threw it into the brazier. The skin was burned to ashes.

The bridegroom had already passed the imperial examinations with flying colours, and the old king had made him his successor. He was sleeping in the palace that night when he suddenly felt a searing pain and knew that something had happened. Instantly he changed into a flying dragon and flew to the third daughter in a jiffy. But he was too late. When the kind and beautiful girl saw the skin burned, she thought that her husband had died, and was so sad that she took her own life. The bridegroom took her in his arms and cried bitterly. His tears became two streams.

The day broke as a red sun rose. Wiping his tears, the bridegroom took third daughter in his arms and flew away. Instantly, they were transformed into a golden dragon and a red phoenix flying in the sky towards the heavenly palace. And from that time on, there are dragons and phoenixes in the sky and a dragon-and-phoenix match symbolizes a good marriage.

Written by Jin Deshun
Translated by Yu Fanqin

Dragon Girl

WHEN Heaven was first separated from Earth, nine dragons lived up in Heaven. They used to frolic in the glorious clouds, from which they could clearly see the landscapes, trees, flowers, birds and animals on earth.

It so happened that one day, when they were enjoying themselves in this way, they spotted a jewel down on earth which flashed with red, green and violet light. Partial to jewels by nature, they vied with each other in rushing down to secure it. But strangely the gem, while clearly in sight when viewed from above, was covered by dense woods on earth and was nowhere to be seen. The nine dragons, longing to possess this rare treasure, stayed on earth and hunted. They went on with their search until they were finally metamorphosed into the Lancang River. This is why the river later came to be called Nine-Dragon River.

A towering precipice nearby was called the Golden Precipice. Under it was a deep cave called Golden Precipice Cave. The nine dragons had a magnificent palace built in this spacious and well-ventilated cave as their permanent residence.

Many a year passed before one of the dragons, the White Dragon, had a daughter born to him. She was a pretty little creature with skin as tender as lotus root and eyes as bright as pearls. When she was sixteen years old, she began to find life in the dragon palace too boring. Sick of life underneath the water, she went to enjoy herself on the surface. One day, enchanted by a medley of white beaches, verdant grass, red flowers and yellow fruit, she forgot about going back to the dragon palace and played about on earth for a long time. Longing to see more, she picked her way along a twisting trail up to a peak north of the Lancang River, from which she had an enchanting view of fields overgrown with towering palm trees, fernleaf hedge bamboos, banana trees and betel palms that rose in slender elegance from the lush fields. The Dragon Girl, delighted at the sight, went on with her exploration until she came to the flatlands. There she saw men ploughing the fields, women transplanting rice seedlings, and kids splashing in a pond with the water buffaloes they were herding. Taken by the liveliness and joy of life on earth, the Dragon Girl made up her mind not to return to her boring life in the dragon palace.

Just then a young man in his early twenties came by along a path between the fields. The Dragon Girl fell instantly in love with this honest, hardworking fellow, who wore a double-breasted jacket, a hood, and rolled-up trousers. His hands were stained with dirt. She went timidly over and asked, "Dear brother farmer, what's this place called?"

"Our plain is called Mengyang," the young man answered politely, "where many people of the Dai nationality live. Dear sister, where are you heading for? Why are you travelling by yourself?"

The Dragon Girl had intended to tell him all about her background, but checked herself on second thought: "Dear brother farmer, I live by the Lancang

River. I went out to get some flowers and wild herbs up on the mountains this morning and lost my way, whereupon I wandered all the way here."

The young man, upon hearing this, said in a kind voice, "Come and have a rest at my place. You must be tired. I have a small bamboo cottage with fine bamboo stools."

The Dragon Girl, pleased with his kindness, went with him to his house, head lowered in sweet shyness.

The young man, whose name was Yan Maoyang, had long since lost his parents, and having had no siblings, lived all by himself in a small bamboo cottage. He had started herding buffaloes for other people at a young age, and learned to plough and to hoe at the age of ten. He was poor but kindhearted, eager to offer his services to people whenever they had trouble. He was very popular among the villagers, and many obliging "aunts" had offered to find him a good wife. But they had failed to come up with a suitable one.

On that day, when the sun had set and all the birds had returned to their nests, the local people were delighted and at the same time surprised at the sight of Yan Maoyang leading home a pretty young girl. They went up on their balconies to watch. Yan Maoyang, though a bit abashed, felt at ease. Why should he be ashamed of inviting someone who had lost her way to have a rest at his home?

On reaching his cottage, Yan Maoyang fetched a basin of water which he placed on the balcony for Dragon Girl to wash herself. Then he laid out a rattan table on which he placed some rice and soup made of tender bamboo shoots and pickled cucumber. He called warmly, "Dear sister, you must be starving after walking the whole day. Come and have something to eat." At the sight of the blushing Dragon Girl, he added quickly, "You might find the soup simple and the vegetables crude. But my glutinous rice is refined and tasty. Come and try some."

"How can I thank you enough, dear brother farmer?" So saying, Dragon Girl picked up the chopsticks and bowl and began enjoying her first meal on earth which she thought was better than any sea food she had ever eaten.

However, Yan Maoyang was getting more and more uneasy. For it was getting dark, and how could a sturdy young man share a house with a beautiful young woman? By then it was too late to see the girl off on her way home. Dragon Girl, quick to sense his uneasiness, decided it was best to tell the whole story. Thus she began in an outright yet most tender manner, "Dear brother farmer, you must excuse me for not telling the truth. But I am the daughter of the dragon that lives in Golden Precipice Cave. I came here out of a yearning for life on earth. Please keep me as your good wife."

Yan Maoyang, taken by surprise, found it hard to identify this beautiful girl at his side with the dragon's daughter from the Lancang River. But the girl kept repeating her story. At last Yan Maoyang stopped questioning her, for he wanted her, be she true or a fake. Therefore he confided honestly, "Dragon Girl, you are as pure and clear as a drop of water. But I am poor, and our life together will be a hard one." The Dragon Girl, though, was adamant: "So long as we are devoted to each other, we will make a happy life even out of bitterness." So they were married that very night.

The next day when the neighbours learned about it they swarmed in to offer their congratulations, carrying fresh flowers, new rice and brown sugar. Moved at the kindness and honesty of these villagers, Dragon Girl thanked all of them most sincerely with palms together. "I am very much indebted to you for your kindness and generosity in keeping me here. I promise to do my best to help you in any difficulties."

At this the delighted villagers all spoke their own wishes. One asked, "Can you ensure more rainfall for us? Ours is a fairly dry area, and it is almost impossible to transplant rice seedlings without sure rainfall."

"We Mengyang people can't swim or row a boat," another put in, "and have been thwarted in every attempt to cross the river to visit our relatives in the Jinghong Plain. Will you help us cross the river?"

The Dragon Girl was only too willing to help. From then on, it is said, Mengyang Plain had the best weather for years on end, ensuring bumper harvests for every village. When any Mengyang people wanted to visit relatives, all they needed to do was call out to the Lancang River, "We are natives of Mengyang, and we want Dragon Girl to help us cross the river." At these words, a bridge would appear spanning the river to carry the people across.

A year later Dragon Girl became pregnant. She was visited constantly by her neighbours, who hoped she would give birth to a chubby, healthy baby. Nobody knew what misfortune was in store for her.

The headman of Jinghong Plain wanted a new palace built for him, so he drove all the able-bodied men to fell trees for him up in the mountains. They toiled for a month and got all the trees ready, only to have them all washed away by the torrents of the Lancang River while ferrying them back to the village. For ninety-nine days the thousands of men tried hard to fish them out, but in vain. They were at their wits' end. Then a wise man went to the headman and advised, "My lord, I have heard it said, on my trip to visit relatives, that a young man in Mengyang has married the dragon's daughter. You will get your trees all right if you get him to help you." So the headman of Jinghong sent someone to fetch Yan Maoyang.

Being kind and obliging, Yan Maoyang was always ready to render a service, be it vital or trivial. But this time it was difficult, for his wife was about to give birth. The messenger from Jianghong, seeing him reluctant, pleaded most pitifully, "Please have mercy on us poor Jinghong people, for the headman will kill us if we fail to dredge out the trees."

At this Dragon Girl said, "Go ahead, dear husband. It's your nature to help people in trouble. I will be all right with our neighbours looking after me." Convinced by these words, Yan Maoyang set out for Jinghong.

After her husband had left, Dragon Girl came to the side of a river in Mengyang and begged the river god to carry a message to the Dragon King in the Lancang River, asking him to help her husband fish the trees out. The Dragon King, aching to see his daughter in distress, sent many fish and shrimps to give Yan Maoyang a hand. In no time the thousand or so trees were piled up beside the bank. The awe-stricken Jinghong people exclaimed, "Alas, it must be by magic! Only a member of the Dragon King family has such magical powers."

The news somehow found its way into the headman's ears. He agreed that Yan Maoyang's ability was really exceptional, unrivalled by all the Jinghong people. At this some minor tribal leader came forward to offer his views: "My honourable lord, your days are numbered."

Glaring at him, the headman asked, "Why? Is there anyone set on murdering me?"

"Not yet," the man said. "But you've got to be on your guard. Just think, Yan Maoyang is a thousand times more powerful than you. If he gets the idea of being the headman of Jinghong, there is no stopping him."

"But what can I do?" asked the headman anxiously.

"Take the opportunity now, when he is not on his guard, and kill him first." The man pulled out his scimitar and gestured suggestively.

The headman, thinking at first it would be simply too ungrateful and mean of him, shook his head. But on second thought he decided to take the advice, for he could not bear the thought of having a Mengyang man as headman of the Jinghong people. So he ordered a man to take Yan Maoyang to the forest and chop off his head. All the spectators pleaded with the headman to spare the Dragon King's son-in-law, for fear that the Dragon King would take revenge, but the headman would not listen. He took up a sword and killed Yan Maoyang right on the spot.

When news of his death came to Mengyang, Dragon Girl fainted. As she came to, her neighbours rushed to her rescue. "How can there be such meanness in the world?" cried Dragon Girl bitterly. "My husband went to help them out, and then they killed him. I cannot just let this pass." That night she went to the dragon palace to ask for help. The Dragon King, furious, immediately sent all his marine forces to dam up the Lancang River with boulders. All at once the water flowed backwards, flooding all the farm fields and the whole village of Jinghong. The people there fled for their lives to the highlands, where they survived on tree leaves and wild herbs.

Why all this inundation without a single drop of rainfall? The headman of Jinghong was puzzled. He had expected the flood to die down in a few days, but ten days passed and the flood still showed no sign of receding. Soon all the leaves and wild herbs were consumed and the people of Jinghong were on the verge of starvation. At this juncture, a wise man from the village went to the headman and said, "This is all because you have killed a good man out of an evil whim. You have enraged Dragon Girl and for that offence you will have to go down on your hands and knees to plead for mercy." These remarks awoke the headman's conscience. Overcome with chagrin, he set out in a raft with a couple of eloquent men. They came to the highland on the opposite bank, and then went all the way on foot to Mengyang to beg for mercy at the feet of Dragon Girl. "Dear Dragon Girl, I've been hoodwinked by a treacherous, mean character into killing your dear husband. It's too late to repent now, so just kill me to right the wrong, and don't flood all the Jinghong people."

Glaring, Dragon Girl cursed him as an ingrate, and asked him sarcastically to give back her husband. This was beyond the headman's power, so he bowed all the lower and asked for mercy. Dragon Girl, after weeping a while, gradually calmed down. At this the headman of Jinghong said, "Dear Dragon Girl, if you give us Jinghong people peace and pardon our crime, we will worship and support you in days to come."

Not having the heart to drown all the people of Jinghong, the bereaved and angry Dragon Girl nodded her head and granted his plea. She set out that night for the dragon palace and asked her father to open up the river course. Next morning all the water had subsided and the farm fields and cottages emerged once more.

Out of gratitude, the people of Jinghong started to worship Dragon Girl as a divinity and offer sacrifices and hold ceremonies for her by the riverside every year. And it is said that Dragon Girl gave birth to a lovely baby upon returning to the dragon palace.

Compiled by Yan Feng
Translated by Li Hong

Sketches by Wang Fuyang, Sun Yizeng
and Zheng Shufang

龙的传说

熊猫丛书

*

中国文学出版社出版
（中国北京百万庄路 24 号）
中国国际图书贸易总公司发行
（中国北京车公庄西路 35号）
北京邮政信箱第 399 号　　邮政编码 100044
1988 第 1 版（英）
1990 第 2 次印刷
1994 第 3 次印刷
ISBN 7-5071-0024-3/I.24（外）
10—E—2301P